Skyrocket Your Business at Zero Cost

SKYROCKET
YOUR BUSINESS
AT ZERO COST

*Make a Difference with
Company Growth and
Community Development*

DR. FRANCIS N. MBUNYA

NEW YORK

LONDON • NASHVILLE • MELBOURNE • VANCOUVER

Skyrocket Your Business at Zero Cost

Make a Difference with Company Growth and Community Development

Published in New York, New York, by Morgan James Publishing in partnership with Difference Press. Morgan James is a trademark of Morgan James, LLC.
www.MorganJamesPublishing.com

ISBN 9781642797954 paperback
ISBN 9781642797961 eBook
Library of Congress Control Number: 2019949864

Cover & Interior Design by:
Christopher Kirk
www.GFSstudio.com

Editor:
Moriah Howell

Book Coaching:
The Author Incubator

Morgan James is a proud partner of Habitat for Humanity Peninsula and Greater Williamsburg. Partners in building since 2006.

Get involved today! Visit
MorganJamesPublishing.com/giving-back

To my son, Evanmorgan Mbunya, for his seventh birthday. Thank you for being my number-one coach.

Table of Contents

Chapter 1

How Can I Grow My Business by Contributing to Community Development?

How Can I Be More to My Community?

Despite the increase in development as a result of increased employment opportunities and advancements in technology, quality of life continues to be a big problem. Unemployment, poor housing, and quality education still remain among the top challenges of community development. This has continually riled up many businesses executives who are interested in doing business beyond the usual level. They are worked up because they clearly understand the role a sustainable community can play in their life and in their business.

1

This also explains the reason why top executives are investing a lot of money through donations to contribute to solving community development challenges.

In a conversation with Tricia, a top executive of a successful construction company, on how she is confronted by these challenges, I learned great insight. She explained to me that she is worried daily about the alarming rate of individuals who are unable to afford basic accommodation and better education because of poverty. She also explained her interest and willingness to be a part of the solution to this problem; however, her busy schedule and demanding job as the president and executive officer of her company might be keeping her from doing a lot. In a long conservation with her, I was able to pick out her value and to suggest a solution, which was a dream come true for her because of several reasons I will share as you read along. Right now, I would like to share with you some of her values, which made her an outstanding executive and her company successful.

She focused daily on helping her business leaders create and execute the visions of her company. In addition to working with the leaders of her company to develop smart strategies, she was passionate about working with early-stage entrepreneurs. She expressed that it was incredibly satisfying to invest in people who love what they are doing. She also enjoyed sharing best practices through storytelling, mentoring, and recommending best-in-class advisers. That was why she spent most of her time providing one-on-one coaching to her business leaders, creating value throughout organisations, far beyond the top line. This helped her understand disruptive forces in the leadership chain of her business and how she could get ready for what was next.

Despite her busy schedule trying to pave a successful path for her company, she was interested in giving back to her community, especially in the area of urban education. Like many executives, she was most excited about working in areas where she could have the biggest impact. She was also concerned about how quick her contribution can actually cause the change she desired in community development. But most importantly, whether she was doing volunteer work or building companies, she had learned that creating lasting change is a lot like running a marathon. Pacing mattered a lot to her. In addition, she was very critical in looking for milestones and her focus was on how to measure progress along the way.

Away from work, she chaired the board of directors of a nonprofit that was committed to contributing to community development. She loved co-creating in this space to lend a hand to the neighbourhood. Her company's dedication to community development ran deep; it was instituted with an initiative to encourage associates to take active roles on the board of a local nonprofit. Many of her company leaders serve on nonprofit boards. She was heavily involved with serving nonprofit and loved to tell her visitors about the work she and her company were supporting. She was concerned about unemployment, poverty, and housing.

She was energetic about community-building opportunities. Every day she would ask herself the question "How can we all achieve greater social impact?" She knew that the answer required putting together a strategy that would improve her community and the individuals living in it. Despite all that she was already doing, she also expressed interest in exploring new opportunities to improve her impact. I knew that there was a lot of information out there and many people were also doing great jobs to make an impact. But Tricia was particularly concerned about how her donation could better impact community development while also adding value to her company.

Like Tricia, many executives and entrepreneurs are worked up daily with the challenges on how they could contribute to community development and hope they could be a magic solution to the problem. They are willing to contribute in any way they can. However, their job tasks are major challenges for them to step up and fully engage in the contribution of community development. Given that the sustainability of their company also depends on how much profit they are able to make, they are very conscious of how much time and money they can eventually invest in solving the problems they might be interested in and still keep their business on the front line of competition. Like Tricia, many executives wish that there was a win-win solution to the challenges of community development. What if I tell you there is a win-win solution? Yes, certainly there is, but first you need to clearly identify what exactly is keeping you awake, what type of solution will be a dream come true for you, and, most importantly, what it might cost you if this problem is not solved. This will help you to see beyond the challenges and create a sense of urgency in your interest. It will also help you better lay down a road map for how you could contribute to solving these challenges and at the same time still being able to keep the interest of your business in front of you.

One of the things I picked out from Tricia's case is that she is worried about a problem she could not really solve. Why do I say so? Community development challenges, including poverty, unemployment, and poor housing, are developmental issues that are too broad to have a generic answer to solving them. Thus, if your focus is on how you can solve poverty or unemployment, you might end up providing a generic solution that only prompts the need for more follow-up solutions. In that way, you will notice that you are continually overworked because you are unsatisfied with the outcomes of your solution. So, the first thing that Tricia needed to do to find a magic solution to the issue that was keeping her worried was to narrow down this issue to a level were a solution could come directly from her.

We can say that what was driving Tricia crazy was not what she could do to solve the problem of unemployment or poverty. Specifically, what was driving her crazy was how she could contribute to solving poverty, unemployment, and housing by donating to a cause that would contribute significantly to solving these problems. Breaking down the problem to a more specific level helped Tricia be able to specifically evaluate how valuable her previous contributions had been and what she could do to increase her impact. This also boosted her confidence to explore more ways in which she could add value to the work she was doing rather than thinking she completely needed a new way of doing it.

Tricia was most worried about how she could achieve greater impact in her business and society while still donating to causes that were helping to solve this problem. In addition, she was also frustrated about the fact that she can only do a little due to her busy schedule and limited donations and wished she could multiply her impact. On the other hand, we can also learn here that if Tricia could have the opportunity to increase the profit output of her company, she would be willing to do more by giving more financial investments. However, in most cases, many executives like Tricia are confronted by the fact that although they would like to do more, they have limited financial resources to contribute.

We also understand that Tricia's inability to find a sustainable solution was the main thing keeping her awake most nights. We also noticed that she was doing all she could within her power to be a part of the solution. She volunteered as a chair in a nonprofit that was working to solve the challenges and also encouraged most of her executive to take up the same approach. These were already great initiatives with high potentials to contribute in solving the problems she was facing. However, the question that remains unanswered is why was Tricia worried about the fact that she was not doing enough? In other words, what was it worth to Tricia if she did not find a satisfactory solution to this problem?

In my conversation with her, I learned the she and her team had spent a lot of money in building infrastructure that could solve some of the problems of poverty and unemployment. However, this also meant putting aside resources that could be reinvested in her business to expand their market and generate more income. Tricia and her team's inability to explore new market opportunities and stay in competition with other companies could be a potential threat to her company. This would also put her in a situation where she might no longer have the opportunity to make her impact because her company might be unable to generate enough revenue to sustain itself. This was because her ability to continually donate was sustained through the work of her company. Thus, Tricia needed to find a less costly and more sustainable way of protecting the interest of her company while at the same still being able to give more to support her community.

What Difference Does It Make Solving the Problem?

Contributing to solving some of the major problems limiting community development was a greater achievement to Tricia's personal value as one of the leading CEOs interested in adding value to her community. Her engagements in community development would contribute greatly to her company legacy and continually promote its brand as the people's brand. Tricia wished that her effort in giving back to her community through the donations she was already making had more impact to herself and her business. If this was accomplished, she would be satisfied that she had succeeded in giving her company a legacy. This would make her feel more fulfilled in her accomplishments. In a nutshell, Tricia's dream come true was to ensure that any donation she made added great value to solving unemployment, poor housing, and poverty in her community while at the same time creating more business opportunities for her company.

In the next chapter you will learn how, based on Tricia's challenges and her dream result, she finally solved this problem and at the same time created more opportunities for her business by simply increasing the impact of her donation. The approaches in the subsequent chapters show how you can simultaneously support any cause you are interested in and grow your business at the same time without having to set aside extra time and money for both. It is a one-stop solution that gives you the opportunity to scale up the results of the cause you support and skyrocket your business growth with the same cost.

Chapter 2:

What Do I Need to Do for My Donation to Start Making Impact?

Being the Difference

I t might not have been clear to me at the time, but the result of one person's donation seven years ago added more value to my life than I ever thought possible. I can still picture the scene very clearly. It was my last year in high school. That particular day was a Monday. I was dressed in blue pants and a jacket. It was a wet afternoon, and the time was exactly 12:15 p.m. It was lunchtime, and I had no money for lunch. I decided to distract myself by taking a walk to the art classroom to talk to this pretty lady I had met a few days back in school. Normally, the last year in high school was the busiest year, and you had to take things very seriously because it was the gateway to a prestigious university, which was just next door. We all did everything we could to make sure we graduated, from wearing the uniform to start dressing up like smart teenagers. The last year in high school was termed "the master key to freedom." So most final-year high school students would spend their break time studying or participating in group discussions.

Because of that, I knew exactly where I could find this pretty lady. At my own end, I could not study because I was hungry and could barely focus. When I went to meet her that afternoon, she was having a good discussion with her friends, but when she saw me show up, she decided to give me about fifteen minutes of her time. Although I sounded and looked as happy as I could possibly be, she immediately picked out the difference compared to the couple of times we had met up.

She said to me, "You look hungry. Why don't we go to the dinning shelter and get something to eat?"

The dinning shelter was an assigned location in school where food could be sold during break period. I hesitated because I did not have money with me. However, I did not know how to turn down her offer because that was the only way I could spend some time with her. Besides I still wanted to keep my pride and not be a "broke" guy. However, she insisted and noted that the bill was on her. I reluctantly accepted the offer, although that was the best thing that could happen to me at that particular time. I still had to spend about six hours in school and I could certainly not be at my best if I went with an empty stomach.

Although she did it out of her generous heart, she did not actually understand how important that offer was to me. She gave me not only a meal but also everything I needed to stay strong the rest of that day and beyond. I am sure that the reason I am still able to picture every bit of that moment – how we walked to the dinning shelter, what exactly we ate, and where we sat – was because of how important the act was to me. I am also sure that she does not even remember all these details at this particular time. That gesture made me to start appreciating life in a different way. I began to understand how little helping hands could be magical and the amount of hope they could bring to the life of people. I think one of the main reasons that moment made a difference in my life was because I was in need. However, that moment also was the beginning of the creation of the value I have today in helping people make the difference they need in any field of life they found themselves it.

A Gift That Pays Back

A gift that pays back is a gift that comes from the heart either consciously or unconsciously. My pretty friend offered me a meal when I was deeply in need. I strongly believe that the reason it left a remarkable memory in my life was because that act alone increased the value I had for her as a person and also gave me the value I have for helping others today without expecting payback. By giving, I understand I am creating more opportunities for a better world. I noticed that the value she created in my life became transferable after the incident. While I was in university, my class had a field visit, and students had to pay to take care of their transportation. I noticed some of my friends were unable to pay. The trip was part of the final course assessment, and I clearly understood the need for them to be part of it. At that moment, I understood the value of helping people in need, so I was able to pay for a few people from the money I had saved. A year after we graduated from the university, one of the students I helped came back to thank me and to share with me how the act had been one of strength she looked to when she felt like giving up. She also told me she was committed in helping others in need because of the impact and the value she felt when she was helped.

Seven years later, I came across that pretty lady again – my friend who saved my day with the magic lunch. Ironically, at this point I was in a position where I could be of tremendous help to her and I did provide my help without having second thoughts. She might have wondered why I was sacrificing so much to assist her with what she was doing at that moment. However, at the end of the day, I was able to share the big lesson I learned from her while we were in the high school and how it created the value she could see in me. This was also a great lesson for me because when she offered the magic lunch, she did not expect pay back. She could hardly imagine the impact that act triggered in the lives of hundreds of people I have come across. I have had so many exciting circumstances where I have been able to benefit from the seeds I have planted along my journey by being of help to the people I meet. This is the same value I started practicing in 2012 when I started working as an executive for a nonprofit organisation where I also happened to be a cofounder.

Small Actions and Expensive Steps

When I started working as the executive director of the Resource Centre for Environment and Sustainable Development in 2012, one of the core values I brought into the organisation was how to create opportunities where small actions could generate great results. One of my goals was to uncover the value of how people could make the difference in their community by being an asset to other people in need. I noticed that in order for me to generate more attention for the need and urgency for people to be change makers, I needed to make it more practical. I also realised that people who have high potential for making a difference are the people at the service to the society – and most often they are entrepreneurs. To initiate how change makers could be of added value to the society, my team and I started brainstorming how "the giving value" could be replicated and upscale.

The results of our brainstorming sessions showed that entrepreneurs at all levels were the primary target to help promote and replicate "the added value donation concept." Our goal of focusing on entrepreneurs was motivated by the fact that they were also people in need of opportunities despite the fact that they had the potentials to give. The question we had on our brainstorming table was "How could we enable the giving (donations) of people to charity work actually give back to their live and business and at the same time replicate the circle?" Our focus was on not only giving but also sustainability.

Before we took this concept out to the public, we did a test on one of our partners who also happened to be a board member in our organisation. He was into fishing and normally sold his supplies to a couple of other companies and individuals. We approached him with a cause (project) we were supporting, and at the same time, we pitched how giving to our project could give back to his business. The main objective of the cause was to support local women as entrepreneurs and a means to mitigating domestic violence. The main challenge of domestic violence in our targeted communities was revealed by field survey to be a result of financial burden on the family heads, who were normally men. The solution we were working on was that if we empowered the women to also contribute to household income, this would help reduce financial burden on men and promote happy homes. When we approached this company marketing fish and asked for their support for our cause, they were reluctant. However, when we showed them how the cause would give back to their business, they became interested in the concept. Our proposal was that we would train the women benefiting from our project as entrepreneurs. In addition, we would also promote his business in the sense that we would offer women who chose to engage in fish marketing the opportunity to preorder from his company without paying money upfront. We put a security budget in place, which allowed our women entrepreneurs to benefit from post-paid services from ordering his company's products for marketing purposes only. He opted to give it a trial and donated. Within the space of two years, he saw great expansion in his business. Many women who started as vendors grew to become wholesalers because of the opportunities available to them to preorder without being constrained by financial limitations. Secondly, he had a story to tell about the cause he was supporting, and this put his brand ahead of other competitors in the market. Thirdly, he opted to expand this support to other needy communities, and this has expanded his business greatly.

It Made the Difference We Needed in My Organisation

Creating the vison of helping entrepreneurs and individuals to donate with a purpose made the difference we needed in our organisation growth. Traditionally, many nonprofits will go for free-will donations, which are most often one-off donations with very few committed in making reoccurring donations through a longer period. When we started approaching individuals and entrepreneurs to give with a purpose, it put us in business. My organisation was able to reach many community members in need within a very short period of time. This greatly contributed to achieving our goals of creating sustainable communities. Secondly, this value brought in the legacy we needed as a nonprofit. We were able to reach out to many people, not only with publicity but also with our actions.

In the second year of our operation, we had more than twenty students from university all over the country who applied to do internship with my organisation. This also gave us the opportunity to encourage more people to donate with a purpose. The majority of the students we accepted for internship were also working on their final year project. Many were unsure of what to do, and those who knew what they wanted to do had financial constraints. At this point, we also approached companies that were working in the field these students were interested in doing their research in to donate to support their field work. We could get these companies to donate because we were able to pitch their interest in the whole process. Our post-internship follow-up showed that some of these students finally gained employment from the company that supported their research work and many of the companies that supported the students also benefited from the data these students generated during their research. The ability of my organisation to find both community development interests and business growth interest in our way of promoting a sustainable world made us outstanding. This was also one of the reasons that my organisation was awarded the prize of best organisation promoting environmental sustainability in our region of operation in 2017.

We Made the Right Decision to Work with You in Implementing This Strategy

It is very fulfilling to me as an individual and to us as an organisation when we are able to contribute to business and value growth. Our value is to ensure that many people are reached and benefit from the whole process. This creates a triple impact in the process of community development and business development. Firstly, it promotes more business opportunities for the entrepreneur. Secondly, it creates more opportunities for the people and community in need in the sense that many people gain employment as more business opportunities are created and many individuals also benefit directly from the support generated from the donations. Thirdly, the implementing organisation also expands its outreach opportunities and is able to reach more people within a short time.

The positive feedbacks we received from the people we have worked with are also evident that this approach offers innovations and growth opportunities for the twenty-first-century nonprofit and for-profit organisation. Below, I share a couple of feedback examples from some of the individuals who have benefited from this model and how it made the difference they actually needed:

"It was a life-changing moment for me to be helped when I sincerely and actually needed help. Before I applied to do [the] internship with your organisation, I was attracted by your approach in capacity building. However, [I was] impressed to receive more than just capacity building [training] during my stay in your organisation. You were able to support me financially in my field research that also provided me the opportunity to network and gain credibility with the organisation I currently work for. All these would not have happened without me being at the right place at the right time."

"Although I have always been moved to do more to support community development, my motivation has never been as high as now. Working with your organisation opened me to not only a new way of marketing but also a way to build the legacy I needed to make the difference in business. In the past years, my giving to community development has been limited to my profit margin, but today my profit margin is driven by my giving to community development. I appreciate the value to create through your model of helping people help others."

Chapter 3:

How Do I Make More Impact to My Business through My Donation?

Making a difference does not necessarily require the creation of a new product. It is associated with the value added on an existing product. However, for you to be able to add value to an existing product you must fully understand the product and the different processes in the creation of the product. In addition, it might even become trickier to add value to the services related to the product because you need to have a wider knowledge of the market and the consumers. In this chapter, I will show you the different steps you need to follow in order to skyrocket your business growth using your donation. The approach presented in this chapter shows how the strategy not only leads to business growth but also improves the scale and quality of your contribution to community development. This also helps to build a strong legacy around your business and product.

Step I

The first step is to understand clearly why you are making a donation. This is an opportunity for you to tell your story and how it adds value to yourself, your company, and the cause that you pick to support. This gives you the opportunity to edify both yourself, your company, and your cause. This first step also gives you the opportunity to gain more knowledge about the problem you are about to solve and the opportunities available to you and your company in the cause of solving the problem. This is the initial point for you to start creating value and building a legacy story around yourself and your business. To position yourself to actually make a difference, another very important question you should ask yourself in this first step is "What actually makes the difference if the problem I am about to solve is actually solved?" This will give you insight into how your support in solving the problem you have chosen can add value to yourself and your company.

Step II

It is important to understand that if value is not created it cannot be gained. The purpose of this step is for you to understand possible ways in which you could add value to yourself, your company, and the community by simply making a donation that helps solve a problem that will benefit your community and you. I also call this the act of donating with a purpose. Your ability to learn and take advantages of any of the strategies I teach in this step will contribute to making the difference you are looking for to grow your business. This step requires you to be able to identify the potentials hidden in your donation, understand the need of urgency in creating value for yourself and your company, understand the different ways in which you can pitch your interest in a process of solving a real problem and eventually understand how you can deliver your interest and your brand to the world through the problem you are solving. It is also very important for you to understand that you already have the answers many of these questions in your business development strategy. What you need to do at this stage is figure out how this actually translates to your marketing script.

Step III

In this step, I will how you how to choose a problem that, when you solve it, will meet your expectations of actually skyrocketing your business. In reality, problems are good to have if there is a way of solving them. Solving real problems is what put all in more business. The world recognises people who solve real problems. People like people that help them to figure out how they solve this problem, and importantly people like you who eventually provide the solution they are looking for. However, for you to be part of a solution, you need to understand the challenge you are helping to solve. In this step, I will also show you how to choose a problem that, when you contribute to the solution, it will eventually contribute to the promotion of your brand. The focus on this chapter is on how you create legacy and how you connect to the right network and the right opportunities.

Step IV

The purpose of this step is to show you the importance of clarity in problem solving and how it translates to business development and growth. Your ability to pick the right problem to solve is very crucial to the impact and result you will achieve at the end of the day. This is one of the reasons you need to be very clear on how the problem you are making a donation to solve will solve the problem and at the same time achieve the purpose of growing your business. In this step I will also teach strategies on how you can find a partner that will support your purpose and prompt your purpose to achieve great value and impact.

Step V

The purpose of this step is to show you why and how you need to understand the outputs and outcomes resulting from the problem you are solving. It shows you how you can take advantage of the indicators and mile stones leading to your expected results of the problem you are contributing in solving to pitch your purpose (business growth). This requires you to be able to understand the "milestones tracker," – the ability to identify success potentials in minus progress and focus on the potentials to build more success. This step also teaches you the strength of looking beyond the problem solving and how to focus on value change and not volume change.

Step VI

The purpose of this step is to show you how solving a problem with a purpose can add value to yourself and business. It teaches you how to be able to identify what you will personally achieve knowing that you are a major part of solving the problems you are worried about. It teaches you how you can create tremendous value for yourself and how this can eventually empower you with knowledge and make you the outstanding leader you deserve.

Step VII

The purpose of this step is to show you how your contribution to solving a problem through a donation can create massive opportunities and help grow your business to the next level. Specifically, this chapter will teach you how you can achieve this by developing a change maker mind-set, taking your dreams across the oceans, discovering new growth potential for your business and finally branding your business for legacy.

Having taken out some time to look at the different steps that will eventually lead you to start making the difference you need to stand out in the way you do business, it is very important to follow through with the details on how to practice these steps appropriately. The next chapter will introduce you to what exactly you need to know in order to start achieving business growth while you keep your marketing cost in check and contribute to community development at the same time.

Chapter 4:

How Do I Solve a Problem That Grows by Business?

Being the Difference

One of the benefits of being different is that you are quite noticeable. Your ability to stand out in whatever you do is a plus in your marketing strength. One way to stand out is by making the difference in people's lives. However, for you to make the difference in people's lives, you need to help them find a solution to the questions they are asking. The good news is that for you to be the problem solver, you do not necessarily need to have the solution by yourself; what you need to do is to find someone that knows exactly how to solve the problem and work with them to help you. In that way, you are better off knowing that the right approach was used, and in addition, it helps you focus your energy in your field of expertise.

At this point, you may be wondering if you know how to solve a problem that will make a difference in the lives of people. The good news is that you are already doing it. The only difference is that you probably have not paid enough attention of how massive what you are already doing is impacting the lives of millions of people across and the world. Furthermore, you probably have not been too keen to think about how what you are already doing to contribute to making the difference in people's lives can also make a difference in your business. The purpose of this chapter is to show you how massive the support through the donations you make is changing the world and making a great difference in people's lives and how you can leverage that potential to create more business opportunity for yourself and to continuously duplicate the great work you are already doing.

You are already making a great impact in the lives of people through the charity donations year in and year out. There are hundreds of good reasons you should make a donation, one of which is the value in giving. It is a great feeling to know that you are able to contribute to solving a problem or increasing the value of the society in one way or the other. Being a giver shows the generosity of your heart and your ability to be a problem solver. There is great magic that happens at every stage of giving. However, very few people have paid attention to the value created and the transformation they are provoking whenever they make a donation. When you give, you do not only support a cause or solve a problem; you are being and making the difference yourself despite the fact that you might not be physically taking part in activities that are leading to addressing the problem you are contributing to solve.

I remember the first donation I ever made back in 2007. I had just started volunteering for a nonprofit organisation as a field biologist, and it was time to experience my first field visit. I was excited and anxious to be part of this field visit because I was working on something I was really passionate about. I had set out my goals for my first field trip and carefully prepared my field notepad in which I was going to document every bit of experience in the field. I remember we left the head office in a Toyota pickup at about 10:50 a.m. We drove for about nine hours to get to the field site, which was a remote village. Although I grew up in a remote village myself, I had a completely different experience this time around when I got to this small village. The name of the village was Fossi.

The first thing that caught my attention was the people's joy at having my team and me as guests. Although my team leader had made some pre-field arrangements that involved communicating to some of the villagers that received us that evening, I found out that the majority of the villagers were taken by surprise by our visit, though this was not because the team leader had not done a good job in communicating our arrival; it just so happened that it was the culture in the village that information was kept discreet. So, my first lesson during my field visit was that despite the fact that the majority of the community members who welcomed us were not aware of our coming, they still welcomed us with grateful hearts and were very eager to learn about our mission and how they could be part of it.

This caught my attention because this habit was quite a shift from what I had experienced in the last five years in the small city where I studied. In the past five years before starting this volunteering opportunity, I lived in a small city where I received my university education. Although it was not quite a busy city, people hardly paid attention to what you might be doing. Unlike the villagers who were so excited about our arrival, the majority of people in the city were normally upset if you showed up unannounced. However, as in normal life, there was a clear indication of the difference in the values of people. This was one of those early lessons that informed my professionalism today: being able to appreciate respect the values of clients. These values were created by me asking the following questions:

- Why were these people different?
- Why will they welcome people they hardly know?
- Why were they so eager to learn about our mission and how they could be part of it?

Although at that particular moment I could grab an immediate answer, I was challenged to look more into the science of community development and to understand the concept of what makes a happy community. This scenario also challenged what I had been studying at university about development. I was made to understand through my education that development innovation builds happy people and increases the standard of living and lifespan in an area. Ideally this should be true. However, my experience travelling across the world has proven that this is not the case in most scenarios. I have been able to learn that happiness is a choice and not a way of life.

This brings me to explore the first question that ran through my mind during my first field visit: "Why were these people different?" In my eleven years of community development, I have learned by experience that if you want a difference you need to be different. When I began to connect to the people in the village, I realised that although they were very happy and wanted to be part of what we were doing, they had their own challenges and activities to do. So, I asked myself the question "Why will this people leave their own daily business to want to learn and do what we were doing without knowing exactly what the end results will be?" As I grew up, I found the answer in the idea that if what you have been doing on a daily basis has not produce the result you wanted, you have to be open to learn how to do the things that look like the change you want without necessarily knowing the end results.

I came to understand that the people living in the community have been doing what they have been doing for decade and have not seen any significant change. Although they were happy, motivated, and contented with what they had, they were very open to embrace change and to practice what look like the difference they want.

"What can we do to be like you?" asked Michael, one of the community members who was about my age.

I asked him, "Why would you like to be like me? You barely know me."

His response was, "You look different, and I want to be different too."

That was one of the biggest lessons I took with me. It has been a guide throughout my career growth. I have come to realise that it is not creating new knowledge that really makes the difference, but it is by doing something that looks like the difference you want that will make the difference you need.

The second question I asked myself was "Why will they welcome the people they hardly know?" This is a question that really got me thinking. People generally do not like to try what they do not know. We are all sceptical about investing in what we do not know when we do not know what the end result will look like. However, I have also come to experience that some of the failures I have had through my career development journey have been because of my consciousness of the end result. Sometimes, I focus on the end result to the extent that I am sceptical of accepting changes that might not look like the path to the result I wanted. We all want change so badly, but our pre-defined actions and anxiety prevents us from allowing our brain to think freely and enabling creativity in the process. This prevents us from allowing our brain to create innovation in the whole process of change.

I have learned that the act of creating magical solutions to any problem is linked to your ability to freely open your mind to welcome new ways doing things. This is justified by the argument that 'if the way you have been doing it was good enough, you would have already achieved the result you needed. The reason you are still considering other ways of doing it is because you need to add more value to the great work you have been doing.

When I finished my master's degree, I was confronted with two options: one was to get into a secure job position with a well-paid salary, and the other was to build an organisation from scratch with very limited resources.

I knew the end results of the first option. I was aware of the fact that I would be able to be productive and to grow in the position and eventually make more money through salary increases and work benefits. In the second option, my mind was dancing between failure and success. One million questions were running through my mind. Not only that, more than ninety percent of the people I spoke to advised me to go for the first option because they thought that was where security lay. By default, this is where the human mind settles. We all want to make the difference but ironically, we want to make the difference we already know. Now the question I asked myself was "If I already know what I want, then what will be the difference when I finally get it?"

After talking to myself for a couple of weeks, I decided to create my own organisation. My inspiration also came from my experience in my first field visit. That community welcomed us because we looked like the change they needed. I know the question you will ask me is "Did they actually receive the change they needed because we looked like the change they needed?"

The desire to be different can only be accomplished if you take the action to be different. Although the community members were open and all wanted to be different because they saw something different with us, I will say that less than 1 percent of them actually took advantage and the action to be the difference they needed. Was it that our visit could not bring the difference they wanted? No. The differences between those who desire to make the difference and end up not making it and those who desire to make the difference and actually make it is in the action. Although the majority of the community members desired the difference, they never took the action to become the difference they wanted.

I remember the first meeting we had with the member of this community. We explained to them our mission and the concept of wildlife conservation and community development. At the end of our presentation, the first question that came up was "What will be our immediate benefit from this process?" They wanted something tangible that could give them the assurance that what we were explaining would eventually play out the way we said it would. This is very true for change seekers. We want to be able to know the tangible benefit so badly that we forget to ask the questions that will trigger those benefits.

When Michael asked me what he could do to be like me, I felt a commitment to do more for him. To me that was the right question for someone willing to make the difference. Like when the community members asked, "What is our tangible benefit in this?" they already put their minds to opportunities that might provide answers they needed in the long run. What they wanted was a quick fix, and what I had learned so far had revealed to me that quick fixes are expensive, and they only solve the challenge temporarily. Michael actually made the difference by acting differently. I opted to make a donation that helped Michael start his dream of being different. Today I am glad he is actually making the difference in his community because he acted differently.

Similarly, I am able to contribute more to the society today because I acted differently a couple of years back. I had the choice to pick an option that was more secure and provided me with the answers I needed. I decided to start an organisation, which has been very successful because I had been inspired by Michael's way of wanting more in life had made me the difference I am today. So, I give because I want to be the difference that many people are looking for.

The Gain in Understanding the Disruptive Force in Community Development

Making the difference in community development has never been easy. We all want to be part of a better community, and we are seeking ways in which we could contribute to have a better community. Community development is one of the primary goals of the government, philanthropies, and well-wishers. However, the big question, which remains unanswered, is why there is little progress in community development despite the joined effort of all the stakeholders is. On the other hand, you may also want to ask if there is something we need to do different in order to obtain the result we want in community development.

Since 2007, I started my career journey in community development from an unusual angle. I started volunteering as a biologist. My main job was to lead a team of other biologists to monitor the Cross River gorilla population in the South West Region of Cameroon. The Cross River gorilla is part of the ape family and is endemic to the Cameroon-Nigeria boarder; there are fewer than three hundred of them living in the wild. You may be wondering what the business of a biologist in community development is. Although I was a biologist, my team and I would hold a series of meetings with the community members before proceeding to conduct our surveys in the forest. This was also important because we needed the support of community members as field guides and porters and also because we needed the approval of the local community people according to local tradition.

What Makes the Difference in Community Development?

During my process of working with the local people, I learned and experienced some of the things that actually made the difference in community development. When we started working with the local people, the focus was on how they would immediately benefit from the project. What would their gain be if they contributed to practicing sustainable forest conservation? Like many development experts, we had a quick-fix answer for them that got them excited.

At that time, our solution for the local people was to provide them with alternative livelihood opportunities that would enable them to produce more income for their household. Our assumption was that this action would make them spend less time going to the forest to practice farming as it was their culture. This solution seemed to work well for both parties at the beginning. However, it was short-lived. As time progressed, the local people noticed that was not really what they needed. Many of them still continued to do what they were doing in the forest despite the fact that they were provided support to practice alternative income-generating activities.

When the desires of the local people changed over time, I began to ask myself several questions: was it that we misunderstood the concept of community development or was it that the support we gave to the local people was not enough incentive to push them out of the forest? The quest to answer these questions motivated me to shift my career from pure science to social science. In order to seek the answers to these questions, I opted to study human ecology for my master's degree, which would enable me to understand the interactions that occur between man and the environment and why certain choices might be made in certain situation. When

I did my master's thesis, my focus was on reconciling the wildlife conservation and local people's livelihood needs. It was the same project area I had worked on for the three years before my master studies. This study enabled me to take a step back and to take a neutral position to understand the main need of the local people and why the well-planned conservation-development action we had was not working.

During the course of my research work, I learned many lessons in community development. One of the most important results I found was that there was a misconception of "added-value" in the difference our development intervention was creating. There was so much attention on the result of the action and less attention on the "added-value" of the action. Similarly, many community development interventions are more action-oriented with little focus on "added-value" consciousness.

I learned about a similar project that was designed to solve a water crisis in a community. Development experts made their research and stakeholders' analysis (gathering the opinions of individuals) and came to the conclusion that the community did not have portable water and that enabling access to portable water would be the magic solution to local development in that community. This might look like a perfect solution if we look at it from the action-oriented point of view. However, it was ironic that when access to portable water was made available for the community members in question, they still preferred to travel miles to fetch water. When a mask research was conducted to find out why the local people still preferred to travel several miles to fetch water from the stream, they noticed that the time spent travelling to fetch water was the only time they had to socialise with their peers given that it was a conservative community. In addition, based on the culture of this community, they lived in small huts. So the only period the couples could have some privacy was when they sent their children several kilometres away to fetch water.

The above example goes to confirm that community development challenges are complex and action-oriented solutions might not be the only ones to solve the challenges. This now brings us to the question "What makes the difference in community development?" The answer is simple: people who are willing to be different. This is not to say direct actions, like building structures and providing direct support, are not important. It just adds that for durable change to happen, we need more than direct action and we need to focus on the people who want to be the difference. When I opted to make a donation to Michael, it looked like that was not the answer to the problem the local people needed. Although this was on a more personal level and a transaction between me and Michael, ten years after the action, he is one of the most influential youth in his community. Although I only supported Michael, he might now have influenced many youths to be like-minded, and they are now building blocks in their community.

Adding Value to Yourself

When I look back to see the transformation that has taken place in Michael's life after I made a donation purposefully to his life, I am proud of the value that I have created not only in Michael's life but in the lives of other people who Michael has been able to inspire in his community just by taking an added-value action. Although the donation I made was a one-off donation, it was the seed that was planted in a fertile soil that has now grown and born many fruits of its kind. Whenever I have a conversation with Michael, he is always appreciative of the seed I planted in his life.

Michael has been a source of inspiration for me and has added much value to my life than I thought when I was donating to him. He encourages me daily to want to do more in community development because of the result that he has created. This is also valuable to me because his reason has help me to develop a similar concept in community development, which is not only helping individuals but also helping businesses expand their market and helping communities achieve their community development goal in a sustainable and cost-effective way.

In the highly competitive world we find ourselves in, we all want to be more. Many people are willing to pay all it will cost them to be more financially. It is a great ambition to be more, but my worry is what difference does it makes to be more without adding more? The value to be more can be created through your purposeful donation. A donation that gives back to you; a donation that gives back to your business; a donation that gives back to your community.

The Need to Market Yourself

To become more, there is an inevitable need to market yourself. Self-marketing has proven to be very challenging and most often comes with a very high price. This is one of the reasons the twenty-first-century market is taking advantage of network marketing to leverage production efforts, sustain business growth, and find new opportunities. The high cost associated with marketing has also limited the growth of many potential big businesses and left them with no choice than to believe they were meant to remain at their current level growth. What if I challenge you today to say you don't need as much as you think to make the difference you need in your business. The good news is also that you might not even need to spend extra money from what you have been spending to take yourself and your business to any level you desire. What you need is to learn how you can create added-value services by doing things you have already been doing anyway. Continue reading to learn how you can make this happen effortlessly.

Chapter 5:

How Can I Add Value to My Donation?

There are many simple ways through which you could add value to your donation. I call this the act of added-value donation. Being able to learn and take advantage of any of the strategies I explain below could contribute to making the difference you are looking for.

Identifying the Potential in Your Donation

Once I understood the concept of potential and how it could empower and enhance the value in everything I do, it became my watch word for growth. Potential is the unexploited ability in something, or better put, it is what you are capable of doing that you have not yet done.

Understanding that there is more you can do is amazing because it gives you the hope to look for how you can do it. What makes the difference between those who keep moving forward and those who get stuck is how they look at the challenge or the task in front of them. Take for instance that you have access to only a single source of income and can make only $1,000 from the source of your income every month. There are two things that might happen in this case. The first thing is that you might lock yourself into the belief that there is no way you can change the situation, and because of that, you budget your life and your thinking around $1,000 and become comfortable with it for the rest of your life. The second thing that might happen is that although you are aware that you have access to only $1,000 a month, you are not bound to budget your thinking to your income. What makes the difference is not the difference in what you have but the difference in how you think about what you have.

This is what I will want you to understand about the donation you have been making for the past decade or couple of months. It might be a habit that you donate a certain amount of your income to charity monthly or yearly in order to help solve the problem, and that has been your tradition or the tradition of your company. This is completely fine because you are already doing a great job by adding value to yourself and your company just by the action. However, my question to you is what if you know that there is more value in the same donation you have been making year in and year out without expecting any reward from it? What if you could change your thinking for a moment and ask yourself the question, "How could what I normally do as a routine produce more results with the same effort?" That is the magic I want you to create here. The potential that is in your donation does not just spring up on its own but is activated by you.

If you plant a seed and you do not take good care of that seed, it will eventually grow unhealthy and might end up not producing enough fruit as it should. However, you might not be able to notice the difference because you always plant your seed at the same time of the year, using a specific method and under similar weather conditions. Think about planting that same seed at a time of year that might not be favourable for it to grow up as it used to. Think about taking out time to ensure that you look after that seed and provide it with the conditions that you want it to grow in to become its best. The first thing you will notice is that you will be conscious of every minute change that will happen in the growth of the seed because you are looking out to see how it will be affected by the difference in the weather. Most important, you will be more sceptical about the survival potential of the seed because you have planted it at an unusual season and time. By doing this, you will be able to pay every bit of attention to the changes that will occur, and moreover, you will be able to find out the reasons why the changes occur. Why did all of this happen? You made the decision to introduce some changes, not to the quantity but to the period of sowing the seed. This goes to show that a simple change in the way you look at something could create the magic solution you need.

Similarly, for you to identify the potential in your donation, you need to purposefully train your mind to want more out of it. You also might need to change the tradition of donation you have been using and move to a new experience or a new way of doing it. Generally, the human mind is sceptical about change, and when change is introduced to our system, our system becomes very sensitive and conscious to what might happen because of the change. This now causes our system to pay attention to any expected change. This also triggers our system to pick out aspects that have been normally occurring in a different and more conscious way. The potential in your donation already exists. What you need to do is figure out how you can make use of it.

Add a Sense of Urgency

Urgency is very important to any system because it creates room for creativity. I have been thinking about writing a book like this that could help people unlock the potential in their donations. However, there was no sense of urgency for me to do it. So it remained on my to-do list for the last four years. The point is that I did not know what I needed to do, and I was unsure that it would actually make the difference I intended – there was no sense of urgency to actually bring it about.

When I signed up to write my book with the Author Incubator program, the first thing that pushed me to take action was the sense of urgency that was attached to the timeline of writing the book. When I listened to Dr. Angela's first video, it dawned on me that I had closed the seed I had with me in an air-tight container and I was expecting it to grow in that condition. That could never happen, even if I gave it as much time as possible. All along I have been thinking that I do not have the time to write the book. What I did not know was that it is because I did not add any sense of urgency to what I needed to do for the book to come alive and be in your hand. What a great lesson! A sense of urgency to is one of the important aspects of productive and effective people. When there is no sense of urgency, little or no result can be created no matter how hard you work. Prior to coming across the Author Incubator, I spent some months trying to write this book, but every time I completed a scene, there was always that feeling that I had not done enough or that there was still more I needed to put in place in order to make it a great book that people would really love. One thing I did not know was that the people who will really love the book were anxiously waiting for me to make it available within the shortest time possible. When the sense of urgency was created, I was able to realise how the book would have already made a great impact four years ago when I had the idea to write this book.

Similarly, when you add a sense of urgency to the donation you make, it makes you see beyond just giving because it is a culture. A culture of giving is great because naturally there are a lot of rewards in giving. Notwithstanding, all these rewards might go unnoticed because the urgency of the action is missing. By creating a sense of urgency, you give yourself the ability not only to create meaningful results in your giving but also to multiply the opportunity and the impact that goes along with your giving.

How to Pitch Your Interest in Your Donation

I know the questions that have been running through your mind as you read have been "What do I need in order to create this sense of urgency?" and "How can I identify the potential in my donation?" This will make more sense to you when you are able to pitch your interest in your donation. The first thing you need to understand is that when you have no expectations, you cannot create a sense of urgency. Similarly, without any expectations, it would be very difficult to identify the potential in your donation. One of the first things you need to do is to be able to identify an area you are interested in making progress in and from there you should be able to create a sense of urgency on how badly you need to see this happen. With that in mind, you will be able to explore how this can happen.

Let us say that you have been looking for ways to create a new market for your product out of your existing geographical business coverage. The normal way to go about this is to do some premarket assessment and premarket testing in order to decide if it is worth exploring the new market or not. In this case, your interest is to expand your business opportunities, which will definitely grow your income and market opportunities. The next question is how do you pitch this interest in a donation giving that a donation is non-taxable and completely a voluntary act? This is very true, and this is not supposed to be compromise. However, I want you to reason this from another angle. The purpose of a donation is to support a cause. The majority of the causes you are already supporting or that exist are focused on community development. Community development can only happen if the people living in the community have better opportunities to rely on. These include better housing, better education, and subsequently a better standard of living. Thus, is it fair enough to say that it is possible for you to make a donation and put an interest task in that donation without changing the value accorded to a donation? Certainly, the answer is yes. If the answer is yes, the next question is how is it possible?

I will bring back the experience I shared in chapter four about the added value I received in donating to change Michael's life. My donation was made purposefully to help Michael be a better person. Although at that particular instant I gave him the choice on how to spend his donation, at the same time, this donation would not have made any significant change in Michael's life if I did not constantly follow up to find out how he was doing and to make sure I provided mentorship whenever needed. I strongly believe more of the impact was in the mentorship Michael benefited from. However, I only had the opportunity to provide this mentorship because I offered him an opportunity to make a difference through my donation.

On the other hand, can we also say that I could still conditionally make a donation to Michael and it would have the same purpose of making him be the difference he wanted? Certainly, yes; all Michael needed was to be different and he needed someone who could help him. Remember, he did not ask for a donation from me. All what he asked was, "How can I be different and make a difference in my community?" This answers the question about how you can pitch your interest in your donation.

We donate to causes because they are doing what we are passionate about. We also donate to causes because we want to see a change in the challenges they are trying to solve. It will be very rewarding if we could improve our impact and if we can see the problem completely solved.

If you agree that your donation is free-will and at the same time intentional, you could also agree that you could donate with the same free-will but intentionally pitch out your interest in a way that it will give back to you to continue giving back to charity. This way, you are able to give both your donation and your interest to your cause.

Give Your Interest to Your Cause

Most causes you donate to have a well-planned strategy on how to deliver the result you are expecting to get when you make your donation to the institution in charge. Luckily enough, the institutions you are making your donation to most often have the human resources or at least the opportunities that influence the change you need. Let's say you are a construction company and your goal is to ensure better housing and education in your local community and you are making a donation to an institution whose mission is to contribute to solving this problem. There are many possible ways you could give your interest to your cause without conflicts of interest.

One of the ways to do this is to create the difference in your giving. What do I mean by this? There are many ways of contributing between housing and education, one of which is direct support and the other is indirect support, which focuses on investment in human capital. Although direct support always brings immediate results and is an emergency fix to the problem, it does not necessarily bring a permanent solution to the problem. This means that for direct support to work as a solution to a problem it must be continually available as an intervention strategy. On the other hand, one of the most effective ways to solve such a challenge is to invest in individuals who then become building blocks of the community and eventually the problem of housing and education will be eradicated when the community members are empowered to be building blocks.

The best way to pitch and give your interest in this scenario will likely be to support a cause that is building the capacity of individuals from that community with the problem you are interested to solve. When you support a cause that is focused on building the capacity of individuals, it becomes very easy to pitch your interest in the process of capacity development.

How does it work? Say if you are interested in expanding your market opportunity to a new city or a new country, what you need to do is to support a cause that is interested in developing the capacity of young professionals in that city or country. Donate to the cause and tag your interest in your donation. For instance, if you are in the construction company, you have the flexibility to kindly make a purposeful donation to the institution by contacting the institution supporting the cause in question and clearly make known to them the purpose of your donation and the reason you are choosing the purpose. This might be tricky for non-community development experts, but this can easily be done without distortion of the value attached to your donation. I cover this in detail in the next chapter.

This might seem like a tailored way of donating, but my focus is on the difference purposeful donation will make in the game of community development. Purposeful donation adds value to the lives of all the parties involve. Firstly, because the donor is aware of the impact and the opportunity it will bring back to his institution, he opts his level of giving to match the impact he wants. Secondly, because the receiving institution is aware of the specific purpose of the donation, it helps them make clear goals on what the outcome would be and how they could use the opportunity to strengthen their network with the donor institutions. A sense of urgency is also created in the action and this enable efficiency in the output and outcome. Thirdly, individuals hungry to make a difference are purposefully targeted to benefit from the donation. This also helps bring in the right people who are committed to make difference globally. When you donate purposefully, you make a donation that reaches your dream. However, this is only possible if you are able to identify the sense of urgency and the hidden potential in your donation.

Look for Hidden Potential in the Institution Hosting Your Cause

The strength of your donation is in the difference it can make to the cause you are supporting. Most often donors are too conscious of the public value of the institution they are making their donation to and end up missing the fact that they might not be making the difference they intended their donation to make. You will agree with me that many institutions that have already created the legacy they need are less conscious of small milestones and are also less conscious of the value of small results. This is not to say they are not effective in what they do. It is only obvious that when you have more you want more and because you want more you are focused on seeing more results and might be less conscious about little milestones. On the other hand, many start-ups have hidden potential for growth and great ability to deliver effective results at very low cost. This is the value you should be looking for when you want to make a purposeful donation.

In addition, organisations with hidden potentials are often more open to networking and partnership opportunities and at the same time are able to deliver effectively. This is because the chain of protocol that is lengthy in big organisation is minimal in organisation with hidden growth potential. Moreover, organisations with hidden potential will be more open to purposeful donation and to work more closely with donor institutions compared to big organisations. The main goal in making the difference with purposeful donation is the ability of the donor to be able to track small milestones and make use of the result at the early phase of the process.

Brand Your Donation

In addition to making your donation with a purpose, it is also good to brand your donation. One of the ways to brand your donation is by tagging it with a milestone you want the donation to accomplish. This also helps you prepare in advance what to donate to match the impact you need. The value in branding cannot be underestimated. We all agree that most often big names in the market sell not because of the worth of the product but because of the value the buyer attached to it. In the same way, when you brand your giving you attached more value to it, and this increases your commitment to ensure that you monitor the output and the outcome of your donation. Branding also helps you in making decision on future donation goals and eventually having a deeper insight of the value of your brand.

When you brand your donation, it is also easy for you to follow-up on the impact of the donation years after the donation and to keep track of what impact it has on your performance. This is a great way to track how the donations you make purposefully are eventually impacting the growth of your institution.

Chapter 6:

What Cause Should I Support?

Understand the Challenge You Are Helping to Solve

Challenges to community development may appear easy to solve. However, the reality of solving these challenges lies in the action process. It is very important to understand the root cause of these challenges and how some of the implemented actions have played out. In chapter four, I presented the case of a community that had a portable water crisis. At first glance, the solution to such a problem is to provide portable water to the community members. In the case of the community in question, this turned out not to be the right solution given that the provision of portable water did not actually stop the community members from travelling several miles to the stream to fetch water. It might sound counterintuitive why someone will prefer not to make use of easily accessible resources and prefer to still go through the "traditional process" to get what they wanted.

Let us examine the case of the people who donated to support the portable water to the community. Their dream come true would be that they local people were happy that they had access to portable water. This would reduce the amount of time they would spend travelling to the streams to fetch water and of course they might invest this "wasted time" in other valuable activities. It is very typical of policy makers to fix solutions for the local people based on their understanding of theories and generalised assumptions. However, they often forget that bricolage play a very big role in the way people think, act, and respond. *Bricolage* is a borrowed French word that refers to construction or creation from a diverse range of available things. This simply means that the actions of people are motivated and influenced by a range of factors including social identity, cultural values, and beliefs. When you are able to grasp the concept, you stand a better chance at making a decision about what cause to donate to and how to donate.

It can be very difficult to invest time in studying what we are not familiar with. At the same time, it can be more frustrating investing in efforts and not really getting the results we desire. Thus, it is better to invest some time or minimum resources to getting the right information than to invest all your hope to a cause that might not deliver the intended outcome. The good thing is that you do not need to do all of the heavy lifting and puzzle solving that will make you understand the challenge you are solving. All the heavy lifting and puzzle solving are already completed for you by this book. What you need to do is take the giant step that will turn your donation into the next big business steps you have been dreaming about.

How to Choose a Cause That Will Support Your Brand

Once you understand the challenges the cause is addressing, it will be easier to choose a cause that will support your brand. This is because clarity facilitates goal setting, and goal setting facilitates effective results. One of the best ways to choose a cause that supports your brand is to do away with the presumption of the right ways of doing things and be open to other ways of doing things.

Two years back, my team approached a renowned recreation facility and presented a project that was aimed at supporting teenagers in remote communities to become proactive leaders and to take lead roles in local development. When we first offered to present this project to the management of the recreational centre and why we thought it could better present its brand, it turned down our offer. The management could not see why supporting a project that did not benefit the centre's interest directly could be a game changer for business. However, after some benefit of doubt, the lead manager decided to give us the opportunity to present to his team how donating to this project might promote the team's interest and bring in new customers. We were offered a one-hour session to convince the team members how they could create a difference in their business through their donation to this project. For me, one hour was too much to show them how this action could create a big difference in what they were already doing.

The first thing I noticed was that they were sceptical about change. They also had fear and doubt about the reliability of my organisation to deliver what we were promising, given that we had been operating for only three years. It was normal that they had these fears. My team and I were confident that we could show them how if they gave us the opportunity. Prior to inviting my team to deliver the presentation, they had been making donations to big organisations and were already reaching millions of potential customers yearly through this partnership. They thought that it would be preferable to work hard to maintain this relationship rather than engaging new opportunities.

Like many businesses today that look for opportunities to grow their market and get more return, the recreational facility thought it could build more market by investing more in what it knew. It is very possible to put in more energy and get more return. However, what if you are aware that the difference you may be looking for can only come if you try something different? It might be very expensive for businesses to engage in new ventures and to try what they might not be used to. I would also like to say that this will only be expensive if you do not take the time to ask the right questions needed and if you do not do away with the mentality that there is a fixed best way of doing something right.

When my organisation was given the opportunity to make our presentation to the recreation facility, we were happy, not because we were given the opportunity but because we had the opportunity to create the difference for both the business and the teenagers our project wanted to support. One of our goals was to serve with integrity and to serve from the heart. Because one of our goals was to see from our heart and not only with our eyes, we could create magic with our ways of doing things. We were given one hour to do our presentation, and like many big businesses will do, they cautioned us at the beginning of the meeting to make sure we did not exceed the proposed time as it would cost them a lot. To the group members' surprise, we needed only ten minutes to show them how they would make the difference. So, within the space of ten minutes, we were able to put a new business idea, strategy, and market into their hands. Without hesitating, they opted to give to our project because it cost them almost nothing compared to the result we promised. We gave them not just an opportunity to grow their recreational business but also an added value of doing what they were also doing with more value. Within the space of three years, they added value to their way of doing business and have not only brought in new clients but have reduced their overhead cost by more than 50 percent.

My emphasis here is that in one of the most cost-effective ways of choosing a brand that will support your brand is to focus on the value and the difference. Traditionally, the main focus is on growth opportunities, which often come with high cost. This high cost can be eliminated by creating value and making a difference with what you have already been doing. It is possible to put your donation to work and reap the bountiful returns when you are able to make the right choice of the cause you donate to.

How to Look for a Cause That Rewards You with Legacy

The goal of any business that wants to be sustainable is to build a name that lives forever. There is growth that is temporary and there is growth that is sustainable. Understanding the difference between temporary and sustainable growth can actually make the difference you need in growing your business. Temporary growth is driven by actions that are temporary and sustainable growth is driven by actions that are sustainable. The question here is how we differentiate between sustainable and unsustainable actions. This question can be answered by finding the legacy aspects in the actions. Sustainable actions are actions that might be performed just once but leave a mark for life. For instance, if you pick to support a cause that feeds a kid, that is a legacy you are leaving because the life of that child was sustained by the meal you provided. On the other hand, if you support a cause that might have some political reasons attached to it, the benefit may only last as long as the policy backing your support. We are all aware that policies are bound to change and causes that are politically inclined have very low chances of earning you the legacy you might need to grow and sustain your business.

Legacy is built around emotion. Generally people buy based on emotions and less often on cost value. The iPhone and other big names in the electronic market have been able to employ the concept of emotional buying to sustain and retain top positions as best sellers in the electronic market. People love iPhones and Nike shoes not because they might be better than the other products built but because of the emotion they attach to this product. Similarly, when you build a legacy around your product, you grow the value of your product and you also grow the product's market. Many people use products because of their environmental influence. Every time I saw a teenage friend of mine, he always had one pair of shoes. At first I thought that was the only pair of shoes he had, but I was surprised when I had the opportunity to visit him and noticed that he had other pairs of shoes. I asked him why he was always putting on only one of his shoes. He responded, "My friends will laugh at me if I put on any of those other shoes." When I asked him why, his answer was, "They are not Nike shoes." His response made me understand the level of emotion people attribute to brands that have made a legacy over time. Another example is Girl Scout cookies (Girl Scout cookies are sold by the Girl Scouts of the United States of America as one of its major fundraisers for local Scout units). People will buy them despite the high cost attached to them because they are buying with emotion.

Growth in your business can occur not only by you exploring new markets but also by you building a legacy around your business. Smart marketers always attach a cause around their business to win emotional buyers, who are more that 80 percent of the buying population. I am a lover of wildlife conservation, and I will buy almost anything that will support wildlife conservation even if it is at a higher price than the market value. Similarly, supporting a cause that could brand your production could bring the difference you need in your business. I would also like to emphasise here that the only way for you to be successful is to take advantage of the hidden potentials in the cause you are supporting. You should be able to clearly understand what I mean by hidden potentials when you go through the next couple of chapters of this book.

You also need to be aware that legacy is a relative term and requires you to think specifically what the term means to your product and to your business. For instance, Adidas and Nike have built their legacy around sport. It might, therefore, be unwise for you to start competing with them in this field. I am not saying that you might not be able to out-compete them in the market. It is possible to out-compete them, but this requires resources and time at very high cost. In addition, your victory might bring you the market, but the legacy will not be there probably because of how you came into the market. Legacy is built around milestones and around integrity. This is why at times it might be much better to look for those who are willing and available to travel the miles with you rather than reaching out to someone who has already travelled the miles and might be too busy trying to cover more miles ahead, such that you would be dragged beyond your pace.

Make Use of Your Ability to Listen to Your Inner Voice

When you are able to see from your heart, you will be able to see what is behind the wall. It is natural that we have always carried away with what we see with our eyes. Many marketers have taken advantage of our natural ability to be carried away by what we see to create huge markets for themselves. True visualisation comes alive when your eyes are closed. A true connection between you and the world can be created only when you are able to see from your heart. Seeing from the heart takes away deceptions and replaces them with reality. Similarly, when you are able to connect with the cause you are supporting from your heart, it triggers your inner ability to be creative and to imagine beyond limitation. Any causes that trigger your heart to want to do more is a cause that will take you to the difference you need to make.

On the other hand, if you are unable to connect to the cause you are supporting within the moment when it is first presented to you, it might be a sign that it might not bring you the result you need. However, your ability to listen to your heart can also be hidden by the amount of knowledge you have about the cause you want to support. For this reason, I advise that you always consider multiple factors to help you make a decision of the kind of cause that could give back to you and your business.

How to Look for a Cause That Connects You to the Right Network

With the continual growth in innovations in today's business world, networking is very relevant for any business to make a difference. Notwithstanding, we have to be careful not to overcomplicate the concept of networking to mean the exposure to a larger and powerful platform. Networking is more about the opportunities you stand to gain through a transaction. Earlier in this chapter, I shared my experience with a recreational facility we partnered with to generate new markets and clients. In my first approach to the creational facility, I did not look like the network they needed at that particular moment, given that they were already making great profit with their business and were happy working with partners they had. After I spent ten minutes with them, presenting what value they could add to what they had, it made sense to them. This connection resulted in a larger network for their business within the space of three years.

What I did was open them to new opportunities that in turn opened them to new opportunities to network. This implies that it requires more than a direct answer or opportunity to make the difference you need. It requires a careful analysis of your business growth, value, and desire from the lens of a development expert to see through the wall and identify the move that will actually make a difference in your life and your business.

How to Look for a Cause That Opens You up to New Opportunities

Opportunities are building blocks of growth and are what you should search for endlessly if you really want growth and to make a difference in what you do. One of the things you should be looking for when you are making the decision to support a cause are the opportunities you stand to gain or create through your partnership. In some cases, the cause may not necessarily have the kind of opportunities you may be looking for. However, to the best of my knowledge and from my experience with entrepreneurs and consulting for nonprofit organisations, I can confidently tell you that many nonprofits are endlessly looking for ideals that will give them the opportunity to meet the need of their cause. Thus, they will happily welcome anyone with ideas that fall in line with their vision. The openness of most nonprofits to accept new ideas and partners is an underexploited opportunity for many potential large businesses to be born.

A couple of years back when I assumed duty as an executive director in a newly created nonprofit, I had to put a strategy together with my staff about how to raise funds to support the mission of the organisation. We had a couple of options on the table. The first was to use 'open' free-will donation, the second was to organise a fundraising event, and the third was to write grant proposals to solicit funding. However, we noticed that none of these options could actually solve the immediate need of the nonprofit to the extent that it would enable it to start functioning in its full capacity. This is also the main reason many nonprofits take many years to be recognised and to be able to compete with their counterparts. Competition is not the main focus for many nonprofit organisations. However, for you to stand out and be able to make any significant impact, your actions need to be valuable and consistent. For this to happen, financial resources are needed. On the other hand, for any start-up business to gain strength and resilience in the marketplace and be able to sustain itself over a period of time, it must be able to break even.

Based on the latter observation, you will agree with me that there is a need for collaboration between two parties that need each other's services to move into the next stage of their business. How does this relate to my experience as the executive director to this nonprofit organisation? I was able to understand the need for growth for both the nonprofit organisation and the for-profit organisation and how this need to grow could be accomplished by a purposeful partnership. With our understanding of the need and added-value of the services, we were able to obtain our first donation that put us to work immediate and within the space of three months we started operating in the field.

How was this possible? We knew a start-up firm that was providing consultant opportunity for small business holders and we had the expertise of working with small business holder, not as consultant at that point in time but as researchers. So, our offer to this start-up firm was to perform a market survey for them and come out with a market map that will help them to purposefully target areas with high success potential in their consultancy. The benefit of the consultancy first donating to our nonprofit was threefold.

First, they will get a tax cut for their donation; secondly, we were not charging them for the any consultancy fees by conducting this research that brought them more market opportunities. The benefit to my nonprofit was also twofold. First, we had the opportunity to recruit volunteers and train them on how to conduct this type of survey and these volunteers were able to conduct them under no very lost cost. Our volunteers were recent graduates looking for opportunities to have some field experience and were willing to be part of this project. Second, the donation gave my nonprofit the opportunity to accomplish our mission of helping recent graduates gain field experience. Given that my team members had the expertise in training the volunteers to conduct this research, we did not have to hire experts. Third, the result we obtained and shared with our partner (who donated to our nonprofit) helped that organisation get data on the market analysis and also helped it launch its consultancy in the area with great confidence. The community members were able to benefit from this consultant opportunity, and this has strengthened agricultural productivity in the community since this purposeful donation was made.

You can clearly see in this example that, although my organisation was not interested in consultancy, we had a service that could open the consultancy firm to a larger market. The acceptance of the consultancy firm to work with us helped us meet our goal of exposing recent graduates to field experience, and the results from the field brought new market opportunity for the firm and more growth opportunities for the benefiting community. You will also agree that there is no conflict of interest in such a scenario. Avoiding conflict of interest is the first priority that should be sought after and eliminated when making purposeful donations.

Break the Routine

One of the main challenges to growth is resistance to change. The fear to dare what we are not used to and the fear to try something that we are not too sure it will succeed. My question is, how do you know that something will succeed if you do not try it? Many people often kick away opportunities because they are too used to what they know and are afraid to learn from what they do not know. However, the truth is that you do not know what you do not know. I am not saying that you should try anything that looks like change. The reason we have a sense of judgement or why we seek for mentors and consultants in life is because we need their advice and expert judgement on what type of change to make and how to make it.

Breaking a routine in your business can be the only step you need for growth and making the difference you need. Most often this will cost you nothing extra. It might be better to say that this might not pose any major risk factor. People and businesses that dare to succeed do so because they broke of out their usual routine and explored something new. This might seem like a journey to the unknown, but in most cases it is worth it.

I remember during my first trip to Brazil to attend a conference, I happened to sit beside this successful American professor in her early seventies. I was in my last year of my doctoral degree, so I had much to learn from her success story. I was expecting her to tell me more of her experience during her career, but she shifted my attention to her early childhood. She told me that she wouldn't have been a professor if she did not choose to move out of the general routine of her community. She said it was a tradition in her community that after completing college you were automatically given a job at the local factory that was just across the street from her home. However, after saving some money from her summer job, she decided to take a short trip to explore the opportunities that were outside her community. After about forty miles in a bus, she was attracted by a beautiful building and she decided to make her first stop to see it. Coincidentally, it was a university campus, and she was blown away by the facilities and the beauty of the environment. That stop alone made up her mind and told her that she wanted to be like one of the students she saw in that building that day. She concluded by saying that if she did not take that first step into the unknown that day, she would still be working at the factory in her community. That is the extent to which breaking your routine could take you to.

Chapter 7:

How Will My Donation Help My Cause?

When you start giving, you start your journey of making a difference in the world. Giving with a purpose can sometimes provoke the domination of self interest in the action. However, there is a way you can fix this problem. When you ask the question, "How will my donation help my cause?" it challenges you to see beyond yourself. In that way, you walk past the self-centred thinking that might sometimes arise. Some of the ways you could evaluate how your donation will help your cause follow.

Find Your Why in a Partner

For you to make a donation that will make a difference to both you and your cause, one of the first questions you should ask yourself is how the donation you are about to make will help your cause. The main purpose of a donation is to wilfully contribute contribution for solving a challenge or helping to meet the need of the society or an individual. Although a purposeful donation fits into this category, it comes with more commitments to both the donor and the beneficiary. Understanding how your donation will help all stakeholders involves a major tool in negotiating the big steps you need to enhance your business.

A couple of years back, a friend was willing to donate a huge sum of money to support the work of my organisation. However, he wanted to be very sure about how effective my organisation would be able to manage the money and what results the donation would make. When he confronted me with the question of how the donation was going to help us make a difference, he was expecting me to come out with the activities we were going to spend the money on and what the expected results would be. That was not too much to ask for. Everyone wants to be sure that any contribution they are making can produce the result they want. In addition, they would also be more than happy if they do not only see the problem being solved, but also know that by solving the problem they could also benefit from the results the action be produce. I did actually answer his question on how his donation would help us achieve our goal. However, in addition to answering his question, I was able to explain reasons why he should choose us as his favourite organisation to donate to subsequently.

How did I pitch his interest in my answer? He was into the marketing and distribution of fish. My organisation had several projects that were running at that time. However, I was able to pique his interest in one of the projects which was meant to empower women through entrepreneurial skills as I mentioned in the previous chapter. So, I told him that we were going to invest his donation to train and empower thirty women to be established as small business holders, and particularly we would make available extra bonuses in the form of free interest loans for women who were willing to engage in the marketing of fish. The free loan was on the promise that they will be supply their first five consignments without them paying any money upfront. However, they would be able to gradually make this payment as they make their sales. The good news was that we had selected him to be the person that would make the supply to the women who were willing to start their business with fish marketing. So when women completed their training and were about to start setting up their business, we were able to use part of his donation to channel more customers to his business. Subsequently, he was motivated to donate more to our project of empowering women because it also meant more business for him.

In the case above, I was the one who help him to pitch his "why" in his donation. However, as a person who is eager to grow, you need to be smart in identifying opportunities that will be cost-effective and even free. One of the ways to identify these opportunities is by finding the "why you give" in your cause. You can also ask the beneficiary organisation how you could pitch your interest in your donation, and they will be willing to help you out so long that it is in line with their mission statement and does not jeopardise their nonprofit status. Like the case I mentioned above, the donor had no clue prior to that if that could be a great market opportunity for him. His donation was still able to meet the objective of our cause without any party being selfish in their motive. This being purposeful about your donation will only help create more results in your cause compared to when you make the same donation without a purpose.

Understand the Act of Creating Better Communities

You might be looking for a direct benefit or an immediate benefit when you are thinking of donating to a cause. However, in some cases the results might not be direct as you think or might be long-term results. This is one of the reasons it is advisable to seek the advice of a development expert to assist you in pitching your interest. There are numerous benefits your donation can create. Let's say your donation is not directed toward any specific cause but is targeted to support the general vision or mission of the organisation you are donating to. How will you know if your donation is actually helping your cause or not? Alternatively, let's also ask our question of interest: "How can I purposefully make my donation to support my cause when my donation is not tied to a particular project?" It is equally possible to make your donation generally to a nonprofit and still find a purpose to attach to your giving that might be able to pay back to your business. At this point, what you will need to make such a decision is to clearly understand the general mission of the organisation. This will also make it very easy for you to fit in your purpose at any stage that might be of interest to you.

In the case above, you may decide to channel your donation to the cause to support the recruitment of a volunteer for the next two to five years. In negotiating the purpose of your donation, you might suggest to the beneficiary organisation that you will like one of the tasks of the volunteer to be research focus. You will also have the flexibility of technically choosing the research focus of the volunteer to reflect the vision of the cause and at the same technically inserting your interest in the description. This could be effective done in a way that does not conflict the interest of both parties by asking questions that can help you eliminate self-centred motived in your donation. One of the questions, which we have seen earlier, is, "How will my donation help my cause?"

The act of creating a better community is often very tricky and difficult to measure with direct results. This explains the reason that despite increase in direct interventions by the state, challenges to community development seem to be on the rise. This is also an indication that other forms of interventions are needed. Donating with a purpose presents the opportunity to make the big difference we need in community development. This is because it creates a sense of urgency. Urgency is one of the driving forces for measurable results. Secondly, donating with a purpose gives the donor and the beneficiary the opportunity to blend expertise. This creates opportunities for magical results that are normally absent in cases where diverse expertise is missing in the planning process of development interventions.

Understand How You Can Create the Biggest Impact with Few Actions

Great impacts are not necessarily created by great actions. What matters most in the creation of impact is not how big the action leading to the impact might be but often in the value present in the action. Let's look at how these two different actions could create different impact in community development.

The first action is a donation of $100,000 to provide five hundred hungry children with meals daily for five months. The second action is a donation of $30,000 to train fifty women from fifty households affected by hunger on skills that could enable them to be employed or self-employed. The first action might look big, but it is a temporary solution and needs to be repeated over and over again for the problem to be completely solved. The second action might take a longer period to be accomplished, but it is less expensive and provides a better way to enable sustainable communities. Based on the two cases presented above, can we say that sustainability in community development could be brought about by developing the capacity of those in need rather than just looking for instantaneous solutions?

Similarly, the biggest step you need to make the difference in your business must be sustainable and not temporary. A quick approach to growth might just be a temporary solution that can only be duplicated by putting in the same effort at every given time that you require the same results. What you want to focus on in growth is the ability to leverage your effort. This requires you to engage in actions that are performed once but continue to produce the same results over and over again. As we have learned from the earlier example, this could be achieve by focusing on developing human capacity using various approaches.

Understand the Unsolved Problems in Community Development

In every marketplace, there are always more opportunities to create new markets and new opportunities. This is the reason that despite the numerous social networking apps and self-help books that exist, development, and duplication in this direction continue. The question you may want to ask yourself is why there is a continual increase in self-help books and social networking apps. The answer is simple. There is constant change in human behaviours and needs. This requires constant upgrade of technology and new ways of doing things that can only be created in a given space and time. Thus, a solution that works for solving housing challenges in the '80s will necessarily not be the same solution that will work for that same problem today.

On the other hand, we can also agree that the existence of a solution to a particular problem you may be interested in solving should not be a limitation for you not to come in as a stakeholder contributing to the same solution. Instead, the existence of a solution should be an advantage to you in the sense that someone has already done the ground work and the work you need to do is to find out the missing blocks in the puzzle. Thus, instead of focusing on designing a whole system completely, which, of course will be more costly, your focus should be on adding value on what already exists. In order to know if you are contributing to the unsolved problem or not you need to ask yourself the question, "What value am I creating or how does my approach differ from what already exists?"

Understand the Science of Incubating Community Building Blocks

One of the most important blocks in community development and in creating the difference is in the science of incubating. However, this process is highly ignored, and this explains why the circle of problems keeps repeating. There is a lot of focus on what should be done and little attention of how it should be done. Notwithstanding, the results are determined not by what was done but by how it was done. When you focus on how to do it, you will be able to see how the results you will create will be different from what already exist. On the other hand, when you focus on what should be done you go through the burden of thinking that you have nothing else to contribute to the problem because it will look like all that was needed has already been done.

When you take a vivid look at what has been done in solving community challenges, you will agree with me that you will hardly notice there is something missing in the solutions that have been provided. However, when you ask how it was done, you will be able to see the difference that can be created by doing the same thing but changing the approach. In the same way, you still stand the chance of creating massive results in your business by simply asking the question, "How can I add a valuable purpose to my donation?"

Think Globally, Act Locally

I am sure you must have come across the slogan "Think globally, act locally," but you have certainly not paid much attention to how you could use it to your advantage as an entrepreneur. "Think globally, act locally" urges people to consider the health of the entire planet and to take action in their own communities and cities. What this means is that the impact of what you do locally is felt globally, although you may not be aware of how this could be possible. Let's look at the slogan this way: someone migrates to America from Africa. He gets a job at a local restaurant in a small community and is paid a wage. He sends part of the money he earns to his family back in Africa to pay the tuition fee of a family member – the family member benefits from the opportunity and is able to graduate and get a job with an international organisation. The family member who was helped replicates the action when he also gets paid.

The owner of the restaurant might not be aware of all of these transactions. However, they are happening anyway. You may also be wondering if your donation is capable of making any significant difference. I want to assure you that no matter how small your donation might be, it has the potential needed to create magical results.

If You Can See It Differently, You Can Do It Differently

The strength of making a difference is in the process of creation. Creation is empowered by vision. Vision is empowered by your ability to see beyond your scope. If you can see it differently, you can turn an individual into a community. One possible way of evaluating how your donation is making the difference in your cause is to focus on little steps that count. If you are able to catch the difference that is created by the little results, you will be able to appreciate how significant the overall impact of your donation could be. Another way of evaluating the difference that is being created by your donation is to focus on how durable the impact of the results will be.

Chapter 8:

How Can I Evaluate the Output of My Donation?

The greatest strength in development (and in growth in general) is output. The greater the output, the more motivated we are to keep doing more. This is one of the main reasons it is important to understand how your input is actually contributing to the end results. In the journey of success, many people quit not because they are not producing results but because they are not aware of the impact their actions may be producing. In this case, they may back out just about the time when their input is about to start making results. For instance, if you plant a tomato seed and a mango seed and daily put in your efforts to ensure that they produce fruits, in the space of a few months you will start harvesting from the tomato plant. It may take you about five years to start harvesting the mango fruit, but this does not mean that the mango tree was not growing. What this means is that they have different incubation periods. You will also notice that the tomato plant will bear fruit just for a season and then dies off, while the mango tree will continually bear fruit season after season. Although both seeds were planted at the same time and went through the process of watering and pruning, more effort was invested in one compared to the other.

This also goes to explain that the more effort you invest in something, the more result you will obtain. What you need to understand is the incubation period of the seed you have planted. Similarly, if you are not aware of the type of seed you are planting when it comes to making a donation that you want to give back to your business you might give off before you start ripping the fruit. Below, I show some possible ways in which you can track this progress and not give off before the result is produced.

Understand the Milestones Tracker

Every step in a process produces a unique result. However, if you are not aware of the results that are produced in the different stages of the process, you may not be able to evaluate if there is progress or not. In the example of the tomato plant we saw above, we noticed that it has a very short life cycle and requires very close attention to be able to notice every bit of transition in the process. If you are familiar with the process of raising a tomato plant, you will agree that every stage of the process requires different actions to facilitate growth and enable it to bare the maximum fruit. You need to prune it and support the branches in order to allow it to maximise its bearing potential. However, you will also notice that the tomato plant might also bear fruit even if you do not follow the process strictly in the various growth stages to support it. The quality and the quantity of the fruit it will bare will not be the same as the plant that was taken care of. Similarly, the mango tree also requires different actions at the different growth stages to enable it grow in the fastest and best way possible.

One thing you need to understand is that if you are not aware of the growth period and stages in both plants, you might think that they have the same growth cycle and period. In this case, you might be expecting the mango tree to start bearing fruits within the period of three months, as the tomato plant does. This will never be the case. However, because you do not understand the mango tree requires an average of about five years to start producing fruit, you may abandon it or consider it as unfruitful after the period of three months. The failure of many investments in business has been the poor understanding of the incubation period of the actions that lead to results. When you are fully aware of the detail in the different processes leading to the end result, you avoid the mistake of giving off before the final results.

The milestone tracker is a table that clearly outlines the different processes and the expected result at every stage of the process. It gives you the confidence that you need to stay in long enough to start receiving the full benefits of your actions. It is very important to have a milestone tracker for any investment you make that requires follow up. It helps you monitor the process closely and to be aware if the actions invested are producing the result needed. It also helps you to be able to introduce any timely intervention necessary for the final results.

Look for the Strength in Minus Progress and Focus on It

The strength of an action is what makes it uniquely different from other actions. The ability to identify and focus on the strength of little actions can be just what you need to make the difference. The action itself might not be something new, but how it is being initiated could be the strength that makes it the difference you need to stand out. One of the most successful projects my organisation accomplished was on music. Although none of us were musicians, we understood the power of taking advantage of the strength on minus progress. The focus of the project was on sustainable lifestyle. When we were at the brainstorming table, the question we asked ourselves was "What difference will our action make and how is it different from what others are doing?" Our focus was to use music to educate the general public on sustainable lifestyle options. Music is something that is very popular, and it requires much effort to penetrate the market and compete with the big names in the market. However, this challenge did not stop us from thinking we could not create the difference that we needed. Instead of seeing the challenge as a major obstacle, we decided to convert the obstacle into an opportunity. Opportunities are created when we asked the question "What difference are we making?"

We wanted to use music as a tool to promote sustainable lifestyles, but the question we had to answer was what difference were we going to make given that none of us was a music star or had any advance knowledge in music. Ironically, that is what makes us unique in the process of creating wonderful results by focusing on minute progress. When you can see the difference in the process it is very possible to focus on that difference to create great change no matter how small that difference may be. So, what we did was add the work "environment" to the music and created a brand of music that was different from what the majority of the musicians had been focusing on. Secondly, we needed to get it out to the world, but we did not have the talent among us to do it. This led us to our second question of value creating (how different is what we are doing from what has already been done?). At this point, we thought about empowering youth through music and being ambassadors for sustainable living. Thirdly, in order to subdue competition and to win the music stars to our cause, we employed them as mentors to our project. Given that their focus was on singing for the environment, they did not see us as competitors. Thus, we were able to focus on minute progress to create the change that was needed in the music industry and to encourage sustainable lifestyles. Today, the concept has gained ground, and many others have been able to grab the concept and replicate it.

Look Beyond the Cause

One of the limitations of growth is the inability of change makers to look beyond the immediate results. There is a whole chain of reactions that occur, and there are way more stakeholders that are affected by our actions than we could imagine. So, when you think beyond your immediate action, you are able to see a bigger picture of your action's impact. I once evaluated a project that was meant to increase water supply in a community. For this to happen, a dam had to be built to ensure that there was enough storage of water at all times to supply the whole community. The dam was built, and the end results of the project were marked as successful and effective. However, the results were short-lived in the sense that the action did not focus beyond the cause. Why was the project unsustainable? The community in question was close to a water catchment area that supplied water to five other communities along the river. When the dam was built, it greatly affected the volume of the water in the period where there was no rain (dry seasons). Because of that, other communities downstream did not have enough water. At the end of the day, they had to stop water from flowing to the dam in order to allow the other communities to also have enough water.

Similarly, when you look at the impact of your actions beyond the immediate result, you will be able to find more opportunities to make sustainable decisions. In most cases, the benefit of your actions might even be out of your action area, but if you are not thinking beyond your intervention unit, you might not be able to appreciate what influence your result might be having beyond your area of action.

Focus on Value Change and Not Volume Change

Value is to me the unit of sustainable change. Early on we evaluated two cases that enabled us to understand the importance of value in the process of sustainable community development. We looked at a scenario of feeding hungry kids and how two different actions could make a difference in contributing to the solution. The first action was the investment of $100,000 to feed five hundred kids for the next five months, and the second action was to invest $30,000 to train fifty women from fifty households affected with hunger on skills that will enable them to be employed. Although the first action will feed more children within a very short period of time, we can see that it does not provide a sustainable solution to ending childhood hunger in this scenario. The second option might take about three years to be completed, but at the end of the day, it provides a more sustainable solution to the problem. Similarly, when you focus on the value of the services you are providing to the benefiting population, you are able to appreciate the difference you are making and the impact of the difference you are making.

Chapter 9:

How Will the Cause I Support Help Me?

The Value to Donate

It is a great feeling to be an asset to someone in need. The value of life is to find your gift, and the purpose of life is to give your gift back to the world. This explains one of the reasons you will find more than 50 percent of people in the world today are not satisfied with the kind of job they are doing. This is because they have not been able to find their gift. A gift is priceless in the sense that the value is from the heart and not from the price. To picture this clearly, I would like you to close your eyes for a second and think about the most precious gift you have ever received in your lifetime. Think about how you felt when you were handed that gift. Think about the value you attached to that gift. Most importantly, think about how that gift was a source of encouragement to you every time you were about to lose hope or how it changed your life completely. This is exactly the same feeling someone in need will have when your donation is used to give them hope in life.

Some of the questions you may like to ask yourself are, "What made that person to give you the special gift in the first place?" and "Why did he/she not give it to a person other than you?" I want you to think about what would have been missing in your life without the connection to that special gift. I want you to also think about how the person who gave you that gift would feel to know that you hold that gift in high esteem. That is the same feeling you will get when you are able to donate to a cause with a purpose. When you donate with a purpose, you go beyond the traditional way of donating and create tremendous value with your donation. You are able to experience the value to donate because you are able to see how the donation is making great changes to people lives beyond what you expected.

The value to donate far exceeds the immediate reason to donate. I remember when I had my first scholarship to participate in a one-month training program in Uganda in 2008. This was made possible by a support from the Tropical Biology Association (TBA), a nonprofit organisation based in the United Kingdom. I am fully aware that this support was made possible by the donation of great people like you reading this book. I can still picture the joy I felt when I heard the news that I was awarded a scholarship to attend this training program. It was a dream come true for me because I could not afford this opportunity if I was asked to pay for it. I can still picture the celebration that came to my family as a whole. I can still remember how I celebrated with my friends and how I told myself this is a great stepping-stone in my life. Truly, my trip to Uganda in 2008 has been a great foundation to what I am today. My success story is built on the foundation of that special event. I have been able to transfer these benefits to hundreds of other young professionals, institutions, and the general public because of a step I took in my life that was made possible because of a donation.

I can also imagine that the people who made the donations to support about twenty of us to participate in that training program for free may not even be aware of how far that opportunity has brought some of us or might have even forgotten they made such a donation because it has been more than ten years. On the other hand, just imagine that I accidentally stumbled into one of those who made it possible for me to attend the training event, and in a conversation he is able to pick out that he was one of those wo actually made it possible for me to be in that training. Just imagine the feeling that would come through the heart of that individual knowing that a donation he made eleven years ago is actually changing the world today.

In 2017, when I was invited by the same organisation (TBA) to Cambridge University for Earth Optimism day to share my success story and how I was impacting the lives of many young professionals in Cameroon, I had the opportunity to meet a couple of people who had been supporting the TBA program. I could feel the joy in their hearts when they were learning about my success story and how I had been able to transfer the knowledge I gained from the program to hundreds of other young professionals, some of whom became executives in remarkable institutions. I was also able to appreciate the value created by these donations when a legend (Dr. Jane Goodall) in the audience requested to have a one-on-one discussion session with me. I was able to appreciate deeply how a donation could create value in people's lives because it has actually created significant value in my life.

This also brings me back to the story I shared in chapter four about my donation to Michael and how I noticed the value it created not only to his life but to many other youths in his community just a couple of years later. The question here is why was I able to donate easily to support Michael? This was possible because I have experienced what value is created when a donation is made with a purpose. So, because I have been a beneficiary of a donation, it creates that value in me to be able to replicate what I have benefited from. The value creation in a donation goes far beyond the primary objective and can create a chain reaction that can completely transform the world.

The Knowledge Gap

One of the greatest assets to community development is knowledge. You will agree with me that no matter the amount of money that is invested in solving a challenge, there will be no result if the root cause of the challenge is not identified. On the other hand, you will also agree that the value of the knowledge created by multiple stakeholders far exceeds the knowledge created by a single stakeholder on the same issues. When you donate with a purpose, you create an opportunity to learn and understand the challenge you are contributing to solve. It also offers you the opportunity to look at the problem in new ways. The value of knowledge is based on how critically it examines the targeted subject. We are able to appreciate this aspect more when we look at how the results of critical evaluation influence buyer decisions. One of the most sought-after variables used by consumers to make a choice about when to purchase a product or a service is highly influenced by the review they get about that particular product or service.

When you make your donation with a purpose, your goal is to critically examine why it might be worth it if you support the challenge. In order to answer this question, you need to go further to learn more about the challenge the cause is solving and critically evaluate if it is really worth solving and also if your donation can make an impact to the cause. In the process and the course of doing this, you open your mind up to create valuable knowledge and possible ways the challenge can be solved from your own lens. Thus, you do not only educate yourself by learning more about the problem and how you could be part of it, but you also have the opportunity to create valuable knowledge that stands the chance to contribute greatly to innovating ways of doing it. The knowledge you generate in this process can completely become a best practice guide for other people coming after you to do the same thing.

In addition, donating with a purpose also offers you the ability to think outside the box in the sense that you have the opportunity of taking yourself off the usual business mind-set for a moment to a position where you evaluate not only how you can make more profit but also how you could add value to the profit you are making. Thinking outside the usual environment has been proven to be a powerful tool in creating innovative ideas that stand the chance of making great impact in life. This is also the rationale behind the concept that taking breaks, naps, vacations, or just simply changing your routine could greatly improve your productivity. Supporting a cause with a purpose puts you in a position where you are able to see beyond your immediate goals and magically add more knowledge for yourself and at the same time create knowledge that could lead the change in other people's lives.

The Leader Gap

Have you ever wondered if you were born a leader of if you are truly a leader despite the fact that you hold a leadership position? This is a question that comes to our minds some of the time when we feel like we are not achieving much or doing much in life. However, I would like to say that some of these feelings come to play just because we often do not look beyond the immediate results that we are creating. We are more focused on our output and less concerned with the outcome. Output speaks of the immediate results you can obtain from offering a service. It is more concern about what you can measure direction. On the other hand, outcome focused on the wider impact of your action or your result is more concerned about what will happen when it is completed. For instance, who I am today is the outcome of what happened to me eleven years ago in Uganda. The output was the immediate results I obtained when I completed the training in Uganda in 2008. When I completed the training, I gained new experience in field skills and leadership skills. These new skills then placed me in a possible where I was able to start making the difference my community needed. What you will notice here is that what I have become today was not the primary object of the training I received in Uganda in 2008. The primary objective was to train leaders who would contribute to making the difference in biodiversity conservation. However, today the impact I am creating far exceeds the benefit to biodiversity conservation alone.

If we come to the concept of leadership, you will agree with me that when you made a donation with a purpose, you are the greatest leader of all time. Why do I say so? I would like to take a step back to what I said earlier about the value of a gift. When you give a gift with a purpose, you send it out with the magic to create beyond the expected. The difference that exists between a normal donation and a donation that goes out with a purpose is the magical message that is sent alongside the gift. If you have ever received a special gift before, you will be able to clearly understand how possible this can be.

I remember a special gift I received from my dad in 1999 that completely changed my life. This gift was not the only gift my dad had given me. Traditionally, at Christmas my dad would normally buy gifts for me. However, what made this gift really different was the purpose that came with the gift. It was a special bag from my dad, and when he gave that gift to me, he said, "I am proud of you because you have been doing well in school. I am giving you this bag because I want you to always put your transcript and certificate inside, in that way you will never lose either of them." When I received that gift from my dad, I magically became the best student in my class the following semester. This would not have happened without that gift. The gift gave me hope and became my sense of focus anytime I was giving up in my study. The gift and the words that came with the gift are still very valuable for me today.

In this case, my dad might not have seen himself as a leader when he was giving me that gift. However, we can all agree that a leader is someone who shows people how something is done and is able to lead them to success. The purpose that accompanied the gift my dad gave me is still leading me today, and I am still achieving great success today because of the gift. Similarly, the support I received to be able to attend my first training in Uganda, which has been the seed that was planted in my life and is now bearing great fruit, is still leading me today to achieve great results. Any donation you make with a purpose puts you in the realm of successful leaders in the world. There might be very few leaders in the world, but your donation is actually filling the gap of missing leaders.

Chapter 10:

How Can My Donation Grow My Business?

You might not be quite sure how making a donation with a purpose can magically take your business to the next level. It is understandable. That is one of the reasons you have been reading this book. I would like to keep it simple and not overcomplicate how this might happen. As I clearly explained in the previous chapter, the magic that happen is in the purpose and not in the desire. Just by donating with a purpose, you have already planted that magic seed. It is time for you to just sit back and watch how the results will be created magically. The section that follows will show you in a simple way how donating with a purpose can make the difference you need in your business.

Develop a Change Maker Mind-Set

One of the inevitable of characteristics for success is change. Change is constant, and this fact requires business-minded people to have a good mastery of it. This is because if you are able to create the change you need, change itself might definitely create what you do not need. Understanding time and change is a top priority for change makers. For instance, success or failure in a stock market business is determined by the ability to procrastinate the change value with time based on the economy. In the same way, understanding the changes that happen might happen in your marketplace over time is very important to plan the growth of your business.

When you donate with a purpose, you are committed to making change or seeing change in the cause you are supporting. Just the act of donating with a purpose leaves you with a change maker mind-set. You are able to see beyond the donation you are making and critically reason the possible output and outcome that might be generated because of your donation. This is a valuable skill you need to grow you own business. The same way you are evaluating the possible results that might be produced because of your donation is obviously the same way in which you should be evaluating the possible changes that might occur in your marketplace and how your action plan can eventually manage these changes when they arise.

In addition, when you spend time evaluating how your donation will make a difference in your cause, it opens you up to look for the value you are adding to the world or to the individuals your cause is supporting. The difference you need to grow your business is in the value your services can generate. With very high competition in the marketplace today, value is what many consumers are searching for. Donating with a purpose helps you bridge this gap. You are able to appreciate the concept of value creation in a nonprofit way. This eventually helps you understand how you can incorporate some of these great values into your marketplace to attract the clients you need. Many consumers buy with emotion. When you are able to incorporate human values into your marketplace, this creates the emotion that is needed for consumers to choose your product over your competitors'.

Taking Your Dreams across the Oceans

Imagine being in business beyond your locality with the same effort that you put in anyway. Yes! This is very possible. You will know that if you have read carefully up to this point, you must have come across the name "Tropical Biology Association in the previous chapter." You will agree with me that if this is actually your first time of coming across the name, you might be curious to go ahead and find out what they are doing and maybe how you could be part of what they are doing. Tropical Biology Association is based in the United Kingdom and does work in a couple of African countries and some countries in Asia. However, your dreams are travelling across the world because of the cause they are supporting. Imagine yourself making a donation to the Tropical Biology Association with a purpose. I earlier discussed how you could pitch your purpose in your donation. Imagine to how many nations your purpose would be able to travel. Imagine how many people would like to find out what you are doing when they come across your name. Imagine how this could make a difference in the value of your business.

The first time I heard about the vehicle company named Ford was when I had the opportunity to volunteer in a project while I was in the high school, which was partly supported by the Ford Foundation. After I heard the name, I immediately went to learn about the name and what the foundation was actually doing. This made me fall in love with Ford cars despite the fact that I had never seen one. Although I was in a community where the majority of vehicles where Toyotas and Nissans, I immediately developed love for something that I had not seen with my eyes. Ford purposely was able to take its dream across the sea at almost no additional cost to its usual business. Similarly, many big brands in the marketplace today have been able to understand this concept and have used it to expand their business scope and lobby for new business opportunities overseas.

You may as well say that you do not have the financial power to do it the way the big names are doing it. That is one of the reasons you are reading this book. What the big names like Ford are doing is at the high-level of donating with a purpose. They are able to use mega donations to create more market. However, my interest is in you because you could use this concept to move to where you could start competing with the big names in the marketplace.

One of the most expensive resources in growing a business is data. When you have no information about a marketplace, there is basically no way in which you could lay down strategies that have the chance of succeeding in that marketplace. Many businesses are failing not because they do not have the potential to succeed but because they are not open to the data they need to strive in the marketplace they found themselves in. Most often the data available might be too costly for them to avoid. All of the above challenges could be a bridge to your donation with a purpose.

Let's say that you are interested in exploring a new marketplace in a country different from where you are currently operating. The cause of investing in that new opportunity might cost a fortune to your business, and the fear and the risk involve will certainly make you not want to venture in such an opportunity. What if you know that it is possible to inscribe your wish into your donation and see your dream come true with no extra cost to your business? I worked with a client a couple of years back whose company was interested in doing business in another country it was not familiar with. The company did not have access to the data needed to make the final decision. If it had to invest in obtaining the data, this might have cost thousands of dollars. Given that it was a small business, it could not afford this option. However, given that we were a nonprofit committed to providing better opportunities for the local people, we saw the need and the benefit of what the company's growth would mean to the lives of many needy households. Based on the evaluation of their need and how it met our objective, we were able to liaise with our nonprofit partners in that country to collect the data they needed at almost no cost. This was an asset to them in making the decision to launch their business in that country. Today they have also expanded locally, and many local people have greatly benefited from the action.

Your Giving Will Give Back to You

Personal development is very relevant in business growth and in creating value. It is about learning to do the same things in a new way or building advance skills to do the same things in an advanced way. When you give with a purpose, you are committed to staying in front of your purpose and to keep track of the progress. Just because you are committed to monitoring the progress of the cause you are supporting, it comes with a lot of benefits – one of which is personal development. You are able to continually learn that new results are been generated by the cause and this helps keep you informed about the changes that might be taking place. Progressive lessons impact personal growth and open you up to new opportunities.

A couple of years ago, I came across a project that I was moved to donate to. I made a donation that, to me, was not really significant. After about eight months, I received a report from the beneficiary organisation about the progress of the project and the results it had been able to achieve because of donations. Coincidently, the data that was in the report was very useful in one of the programs that my organisation was developing. We were able to obtain great insight from the report that facilitated the setup of our program. I can say that the program was more successful because we were able to apply the lessons that came from the data in the report.

Potential Discovery

Donating with a purpose offers you the opportunity to explore new potentials that normally you might not be aware about. Potentials are unexploited opportunities, and they can only be open to you if you are open to new learning and to new knowledge. One of the first steps to making a donation with a purpose is to learn about the cause you are donating to. In most scenarios, the cause will likely be outside their area of expertise or business. However, investing the time to learn about the cause and at the same time reflecting on how your purpose can fit in open you up to discover both new knowledge and new opportunities.

Brand Marketing

Increase in competition has in turn imposed cost in marketing and advertisement. Marketing and advertisement are very important tools of growth. Their cost can be highly minimised when you donate with a purpose. However, you have to be very conscious of the fact that your primary purpose is not to brand market as this might lead to conflicting interests in your donation. The main purpose is for you to support the cause you are interested in and the secondary purpose is to inscribe your own purpose in the process to create more value to your donation.

One of the best ways in marketing your brand through your donation is to invest in community building blocks. Community building blocks are individuals or nonprofits that have high impact in community development. When you invest in them, the individuals within their network have high potentials of taking the message of your product unconsciously far beyond your imagination. I earlier gave my example of the how I first came to learn about Ford and why I became emotionally attached to Ford. If you are not aware of Ford's success, it is probably because they have taken advantage of the strength of market attached to giving with a purpose.

Brand Trust

People trust what they value. No matter how good your product may be, it might not be able to match its value until you are able to make people see the value in it. Most successful businesses create the value of their product through telemarketing or online marketing. This leaves them with the chance of attracting about 5 percent of the people who might come across the advert. However, high product value can be created through valuable relationships. You will agree with me that you will definitely pay more attention to a recommendation from someone you trust than follow what a market advert might be saying.

In addition, for you to build trust, one of the things you must consider is sustainability or longevity. By supporting a course you trust, you have the opportunity to not only market a product but also share the vison of your product to your target audience. This magically creates the sustainable market you need to stay in business.

Recently, I was privileged to work with a company in pitching one of its products. The company produces yoghurt. Our goal was to promote this product as an outstanding brand for the local market. In the pitching process, we were able to pitch our goal to make the yoghurt brand an outstanding and people's brand by identifying a nonprofit that help to feed kids. The nonprofit incorporated the yoghurt brand in its public campaign, whose main goal was to stop infant malnutrition. The campaign targeted about five thousand households. The year after the company started this purposeful collaboration with the nonprofit organisation, it saw significant growth, not only in its market network but also in the number of local businesses willing to do business with the company. All of these opportunities were possible because it marketed itself as a major contributor to community development through its commitment to help solve malnutrition challenges.

Chapter 11:

What Makes the Difference When I Donate with a Purpose?

Leveraging Your Effort

I magine doing a task once and getting the returns over and over again. Yes, that is what making a donation with a purpose does for you. When you donate with a purpose, what you are doing is leveraging your effort. You trigger a circle of like-minded people. You provide the opportunity for individuals who are hungry to make a change in their life and in the world at large. Imagine that you are very busy executive in your company, and your company is in construction work; however, you are passionate about solving the problems of poverty,

119

unemployment, and better education in your community. If you are committed to do that work by yourself, how much work can you get done within the space of five years? To be practical, although you may have the time to volunteer and to contribute to solve the problem in one way or the other, you can do very little within five years given your individual effort. Secondly, because you can only do so much, the problem will continually keep you awake all night. This will also have a big impact on your performance as an executive in your company.

On the other hand, let's look at it from the angle where you are able to make a donation with a purpose that also gives back to you. The first benefit you will get from doing this is that you will be able to convert the time you use to spend volunteering into more productive time in your company. The second benefit you will get is that you will be able to have a peaceful sleep at night knowing that someone else who is qualified is working full time to solve the challenge that had been keeping you awake. How is this possible? When you donate with a purpose that gives back to you, there are two things that are involved. The first thing is that you place your overall interest in understanding the problem you are worried about and how your donation will contribute to solve the problem. The second thing is that you also pay particular attention to opportunities that could enable the cause to give back to you. Your ability to clearly understand the challenge the cause is solving and pitch your own interest in the process of solving the cause pushes you to think critically. At the end of the day, you are able to attain advance knowledge in the whole process. That is where the magic of leveraging your effort comes into play.

For you to be able to leverage your effort, you need to be aware of how the initial steps will eventually duplicate and circle back to you. In addition, you need to be able to understand how the different people who will be involved in the whole process have general knowledge that will not only be beneficial to the cause but also beneficial to you. We have discussed some possible ways of how you can pitch your interest in a cause in the previous chapters. Thus, at the end of the day, you do not have people working only for the cause but you also have people working for you. Just the fact that you are able to leverage your efforts is a major reward to solving the problem you are worried about. In addition, since you have enabled your cause to also give back to you, this also plays a major role in improving the productivity of your company and your ability to continually give back to your cause.

The Value in Time Management

Time management is one of the top challenges in achieving effective results. Your ability to effectively manage your time well is very relevant for your top performance. When you donate with a purpose that gives back, you help to increase both human and financial resources. You increase human resources by employing other individuals who have more understanding and knowledge to the problem you are worried about to put more effort in solving the problem. Increase in human resources in solving the same challenge means more work done within the same time compare to when you had to do it on your own. Secondly, you increase financial resources by adding the value of financial equivalence needed to solve the problem. Thus, there are possibilities that the problem might be solved in less time compared to when you had to do it on your own.

Creation of Urgency

Urgency promotes prompt action. The need for urgency is better understood when the purpose for action is clearly define. When there is no purpose, the need for urgency is missing. When you donate with a purpose that gives back, you create urgency to both the cause that the donation is solving and the need for the results that will come back to you. You will agree with me that for effective growth to be possible, timeliness in results is very important. The earlier you get the results you are looking for, the faster you are able to move ahead to the next level. In addition, urgency helps improve effectiveness.

When there is a sense of urgency, there is limitation on flexibility with budget lines and deadlines. Thus, more time is invested to ensure that the process leading to the results is efficient and capable of minimising errors.

Let's say, for instance, you are in a road construction business and you are interested in promoting your brand in a particular country because you are looking forward for a future business opportunity in that country. In order to achieve these results, you decided to donate to a project in that country that supports sustainable consumption of forest resources. You purpose in donating to this project is twofold. First, environmental protection is an urgent problem that needs to be solved and many people identify with that fact. By donating to this project, you are also building the trust in your brand by scripting the fact that you value the environment in your way of doing business. Second, your purpose will also be to select a project that focuses on using publicity as a means to sensitise the public on consumption of sustainable forest resources. You will also notice that because you have a purpose for doing this, you need a time frame in which you need the results to be accomplished. This creates a sense of urgency and therefore improves efficiency in the process and effectiveness in the output and outcome. This is both beneficial to the cause in the sense that it is able to reach more people in its campaign, and at the same time you are helping achieve the results of sustainable consumption of forest resources faster.

Creation of Consciousness

When purpose is clearly defined, consciousness is also created. When there is no purpose, consciousness is weakened or missing. When you make a donation with a purpose, it helps you bypass the problem and meet the solution to the problem. How is consciousness created along this process? Let us look at the situation above where you make a donation to support the promotion of sustainable consumption for forest resources in a country you are interested in doing business with. Let's say you were not interested in business in that country, but you still make your donation anyway because you are interested in promoting sustainable consumption of forest resources. You will notice that because you are not conscious of the results that your donation can produce, you will pay less attention to what is happening. In addition, the organisation that you donated to might not even see the need to displace your logo in their public campaign because your interest was not pitch in the donation. They might also redirect your donation for administrative costs because it is part of the chain in solving the same problem. However, you will also notice that the campaign will still be going on at the same cost if you pitch your interest or not. In other words, pitching your interest does not in any case increase the cause attributed in solving the problem but instead adds a conscious need for the cause to achieve the intended results.

The Need for Sustainability

Sustainability is empowered by its ability to trigger the action to generate benefit beyond the target population and also have the ability to continuously trigger further benefit. When you make your donation with a purpose, you share critical knowledge to stakeholders who are implementing your cause and are also transferring it to the beneficiaries. Knowledge transfer is a very powerful tool and variable that enables sustainability. In most cases, for the action that is required to complete the execution of your cause, capacity building is required. In 2008, when I had the opportunity to receive training in Uganda, I am convinced that the donor was worried about the unsustainable consumption of tropical forest resources and needed an answer to this problem. I am also convinced that he chose to make a donation to the Tropical Biology Association (the organisation that offered me the opportunity to receive the training) because he was probably aware that it had the capacity to solve the problem. The Tropical Biology Association, like many change-making organisations, clearly understands the strength of capacity building in providing sustainable solutions to such challenges. Today, apart from the fact that I have been instrumental in the success of numerous projects that contribute to the protection of the environment, I have also transferred the capacity I received to hundreds of like-minded young professionals who are now making the difference globally.

The sustainability of donating with a purpose goes beyond the benefit to primary beneficiary and to create an environment where like-minded people are also inspired to do the same thing. In chapter four I gave an example of working with a consulting company to create new market opportunities. This action not only benefited the company and the community that were involved but also inspired like-minded companies to take advantage of the opportunity to reach new markets and grow their businesses.

We have also seen in the previous examples that the action of donating with a purpose that give back to you is empowered by a system that triggers duplication of the action. The action is duplicated through various means. First, duplication occurs because the concept has proven to be results-oriented and beneficial to the stakeholders involved. Thus, many stakeholders are also taking up the challenge of replicating the concept. Second, the fact that the cause has the potential to give back to the donor encourages the donor to continue giving back to the cause. This repeated circle of giving duplicates the effort needed to attain a sustainable way of solving the challenge.

The Value in Resource Management

One of the strengths of donating with a purpose that gives back is the value the donation has in promoting resource management. You will agree with me the cost of executing activities that lead to solving a particular challenge in a society is more cost-effective compared to when the same problem had to be solved by a for-profit organisation. The nonprofit interest of the implementing organisation solicits and takes advantage of voluntary skills, which most often come with almost no cost attached to them. This approach offers great value to both human resources and financial resources and still maintains the ability of achieving a very high-quality outcome.

Chapter 12:

Conclusion

It Feels Great to Be the Difference

One of the greatest desires of people who want to make a difference in whatever they do is to feel great about doing it and have the results they need. The inability to achieve the results that we need in life keep many people disturbed. This has a negative impact on productivity. One of the key lessons in this book is that what keeps many people who are committed to serving for a better world disturbed is not the fact that they are not doing anything. It is the fact that they are unable to generate the feeling that what they are doing is not actually making the difference they want. This often comes as a result of not knowing exactly what to do with the potentials they already have. This leaves them feeling that they need to do more if they have to achieve more. Although this might be true in some cases, in many cases this is not. As illustrated in this book, what we need most of the time to have the results we need is to add a purpose to what we are already doing. However, this also requires the knowledge of how and where to pitch our purpose in order to generate the right results.

The feeling that we might not be contributing enough to what we are passionate about can be a stumbling block in our productivity. This creates loopholes in our lives that can be filled only if we find a convincing solution. This satisfaction immediately shows up when we take an advanced step in doing the things we are already doing. There is a magical transformation in knowing that you are capable of doing something more without actually changing your usual habits. This creates the feeling of being the difference, which is a dream come true for great people like you who are committed to adding value to their communities and the world at large through their support. In addition, the feeling of safety is also generated when you are aware that you are doing something that is actually making an impact. Safety gives you the strength you need to continue the great work you are already doing. Value is created when we are confident of our feelings. When you opt to donate with a purpose, you opt to create safety and value, which eventually lead you to being and making the difference you desire.

We also learned from chapter two that most often the difference we need does not necessarily come from giant steps but from small but expensive steps. It starts with your ability to find the value in you and how that value can be transferred to others either consciously or unconsciously. When you are able to discover the value in you, it is the beginning of a new dawn in making the difference you need both for yourself and your business. However, we also saw that although this might be as simple and straightforward as possible, it requires that you are fully aware of the value of your services and the right strategies to make this value come alive fully.

We learned in chapter three that making the difference does not necessary require the creation of a new product or the development of a new way of doing things. It is more associated to your ability to add value to what already exist. The good news is that most of these values already exist. The problem is that you have not actually put down a strategy to harness that value. Good enough, we have been able to explore various ways through which we can bring out and magnify the values in what you are doing to work to your advantage. Although this might be tricky at times, the challenge can be bridged by improving your knowledge of existing values and at the same time exploring opportunities that can create more values.

We learned that value creation requires simplicity and simplicity is created by structures. Thus, the first step in making a donation that makes the difference is to understand clearly why you are making a donation. We learned that when you are able to find your personal reasons in what you are doing, you place yourself ahead of challenges and failure. In addition, understanding the reasons for your action gives you the opportunity to gain more knowledge on the problem you are committed to solving. This is also one of the initial steps in value creation. It is also important to understand that if value is not created it cannot be gained. It is worth it that you invest in opportunities that contribute to creating value and continually strive to be the difference and to make a difference through your donation. We also emphasised in this book that it is very important to be able to identify the potentials in your donation, understand the need of urgency in creating value, understand the different ways in which you can pitch your interest with your donation, and eventually understand how you can in script your interest and your brand in your donation.

The first chapters emphasised the value of choosing a cause that meets the need of your donation. This requires you to understand the challenge you are helping solve through your donation and also requires you have clear knowledge of the potential market of your product. This plays a key role in guiding you on what cause to support in respect to the growth you are interested in seeing in your marketplace. When you are clear about the challenges you are helping to solve, you are ready to strategically make the choice of whom to send the donation to. However, we also put emphasis on the fact that making a choice of whom to send your donation to requires that you also clearly understand their mission and vision and the specific role your donation will play in solving the problem you are concerned about. Having all of this knowledge will enable you to understand how you can create the biggest impact with little actions using your donation. This also helps you see beyond the immediate benefit of your actions.

In chapter five we discussed that clearly understanding what the expected outputs and outcomes resulting from the cause you are supporting are helps you correctly pitch your interest. Understanding the expected outputs and outcomes helps you take advantage of the indicators and milestones that lead to your expected results. This requires that you understand the milestone indicators, look for the strength in minor progress and focus on it, see beyond the cause you are supporting, and focus on value change and not volume change. In addition, we also showed that your ability to identify what you will personally achieve from making a donation with a purpose can create tremendous values in your life, empower you with knowledge, and make you an outstanding leader. Furthermore, your personally growth in value and knowledge offer the chance to bring massive opportunities you need to take your business to the next level. Specifically, this is illustrated in chapter seven by showing you how you can develop a change maker mind-set that will take your dreams across the oceans. Making a donation with a purpose is actually the gateway that opens you up to discover your growth potential in your business and helps you build the legacy and branding for your business to succeed.

Why I Wrote This Book

If there is one thing I always want to be, it is the difference. I realised that in order to be the difference you want, you need to create the difference. Since 2007, when I started my career journey as a community developer, specifically working with local people and helping them manage their natural resources for their benefit, I have learned a lot from my interactions with diverse groups of people from different continents of the world. I noticed that everyone is unique and that there is no general solution to the same problem in different places. No matter how similar or identical a problem may be, so long as the environment and the people involved differ, a different strategy is likely required to solve the challenges. However, I also noticed that most solutions are not fixed but are crafted in the cause of spending time to understand the real challenge. My understanding of this concept pushed me to notice the specific differences in individuals and to start paying keen attention to what actually made the difference.

With time, I came to figure out that the main difference in people lies in their values. Some people place their values in certain things and others in other things. When I realised that value is what actually makes people who they are, it made more sense to me why similar people having the same issues might need different solutions. This also helped me grow in my career and most especially in networking with people. When I network with people, I focus on their values and how I can add more value to what they already value. This really makes the difference in everything I do. I noticed that to change people, you do not need to create new ways of doing things but to add value to what they are already doing anyway.

My inspiration in writing this book is also drawn from the value-added approach that has been my guiding angel throughout my career. I have been able to use this approach to help hundreds of young professions and institution through my training and mentorship programs. When I started my own nonprofit organisation in 2012 with the goal of helping local institutions benefit from the knowledge of value creation, I realised that the more I implemented this value-added approach, the more positive results I achieve. The approach was simple to duplicate and to upscale. Thinking beyond this approach and how I could make a difference in the world, I thought of writing a book. In my first attempts of writing, I thought it was more of a general problem than a specific problem. So, I started by thinking that if I could write a book that trained people on how to change their mind-set, then I could achieve my results of actually making a difference in people's lives. This might be true somehow, but I also noticed along the way that writing a book that is generic put me in a position where I am of the thought that every problem has the same solution. This is actually not true.

My quest to actually make the difference and to put this book into many people's hands came alive within the space of three minutes in an encounter with Dr. Angela on a Zoom video conversation. My idea moved from general to solving a real need in today's profit and nonprofit worlds. In this book, I look for value to add to the usual collaboration that exists between for-profit and nonprofit institutions. I explore how this relationship can make a difference in their business, community building, and individual lives. My book helps answer the key question "What if you know that what you do usually without expecting a reward could actually bring multiple rewards to you?" I illustrate in this book how donations could actually be more than just donations. I have used this knowledge and approach to create the difference in the lives of many young entrepreneurs and local institutions and for community development in general. I also noticed that my story could make a difference to multiple institutions and individuals across the globe simultaneously with very little resources needed just by sharing my little secrets. It is quiet fulfilling to know that I could teach people through this book to make the difference they always sought using the resources they already have and are already using for the same purpose. The difference I bring is just to show them how they could add value to what they are already doing anyway.

I also wrote this book because the knowledge is not only for entrepreneurs, community developers, and local institutions; it can greatly benefit well-established institutions and individuals seeking to be the difference in their own space. I am aware that we all seek to live a life worth emulating, and we are all seeking for ways to live a life of legacy. It's quite fulfilling and satisfactory knowing that you are capable of helping other people make a difference. This book shows you how to do that. Everyone is capable of adding value to his/her life and at the same time adding value to hundreds of people worldwide. The only difference is to know how to do it.

I am so happy that you had the chance to read this book. I strongly believe that at this point you are well equipped with the knowledge and the steps to start making the difference in yourself and the world. I have also created a platform through my organisation that can facilitate this process and walk you through the different steps with ease. It is time to create valuable change without necessarily spending millions of dollars. We all need to feel better and to leave the world better than we met it. The chance to be part of the global change is here and you can do more than what you expect. Take that brave step today and be part of the change makers in the world by not only reading a copy of this book but by also taking an actionable step.

Acknowledgements

I want to thank my wife, Loveline Mbunya, for always believing in me and supporting me to attain higher heights in my success journey. I couldn't ask for anything more than you for a wife. Thank you to my mum for the great work she does by taking care of my kids. Thank you to my kids – Evanmorgan, Lizzy, and Frances – for always believing in me.

Thank you to all of you who have been a part of my career life in one way or the other.

Your support has been very instrumental in every step I make in life.

Thank you to Angela Lauria and The Author Incubator's team, as well as to David Hancock and the Morgan James Publishing team for helping me bring this book to print.

Thanks for Reading

T hank you for reading my book. As an appreciation for reading this book, I would like to offer you a free master class on how create massive growth and value for your business and yourself. To get access to this masterclass, email me for your link to access it.

You can also start in contact with me for more great tips on how to grow your business by following me on my social media pages:

LinkedIn: https://www.linkedin.com/in/mnkemnyi/
Facebook: https://www.facebook.com/thembunyashub/
Email: nmbunyaf@gmail.com

About the Author

D r. Francis Mbunya holds a doctoral degree in development studies. For over twelve years he has committed his time to support the community development goals in his local community and beyond. His career journey can be traced to 2006, when he started volunteering in the nonprofit sector, where he helped local community members develop their potential on the use of forest resources.

Dr. Mbunya's love of promoting community development motivated the choice of study for his master's and doctoral degrees. At the master degree level, he studied human ecology, which focuses on understanding the complex relationship between humans and the environment and how they can benefit from each other. At the doctoral degree level, he studied development studies, which focuses on how individuals and institutions can leverage the social connection they situate themselves in to grow their purpose.

Professionally, Dr. Mbunya has worked with several for-profit and nonprofit organisations. In most parts of his career journey, he has acted as a consultant to both for-profit and nonprofit institutions with the goal of establishing opportunities that create mutual benefits between both parties. In addition, he has contributed to the training and establishment of more than two hundred small business owners in the last five years. His ultimate goal is to create more impact in community development by establishing more opportunities that bring added value to entrepreneurs and community members.

Dr. Mbunya is also a passionate public speaker, a career development coach, and a life coach. He spends most of his time grooming young professionals by sharing his career journey and lessons learned with them. He seizes every bit of opportunity he has to add value to people's lives. He is fulfilled when he leaves people happier than he found them.